The New Republic

A Commentary on Book I of More's *Utopia*
Showing Its Relation to Plato's *Republic*

COLIN STARNES

Wilfrid Laurier University Press

Canadian Cataloguing in Publication Data

Starnes, Colin.
   The new republic

Includes bibliographical references.
ISBN 0-88920-978-2

1. More, Thomas, Sir, Saint, 1478-1535.   Utopia.
2. More, Thomas, Sir, Saint, 1478-1535.   Criticism
and interpretation.   3. Plato.   Republic.   4. Plato –
Criticism and interpretation.   5. Plato – Influence –
More.   I. Title.

HX810.5.Z6S77 1989   321′.07   C89-090688-2

Copyright © 1990

WILFRID LAURIER UNIVERSITY PRESS
Waterloo, Ontario, Canada   N2L 3C5

Cover design by Rick McLaughlin

Printed in Canada

Cover: Map of the Island of Utopia, from Thomas More's Utopia (1516).
   Reproduced courtesy of the Henry W. and Albert A. Berg Collections, The New
   York Public Library, Astor, Lenox and Tilden Foundations.

CONTENTS

iii

AUTHOR'S NOTE

Unless otherwise indicated, all references to *Utopia* and its accompanying letters, etc. are the page/line references from Volume 4 of *The Complete Works of St. Thomas More*, edited by Edward Surtz, S.J. and J. H. Hexter, New Haven, Yale University Press, 1965 (hereafter Yale). For Plato, I have used the translations in *The Collected Dialogues of Plato*, edited by Edith Hamilton and Huntington Cairns, Bollingen Series LXXI, Princeton, Princeton University Press, 1961, giving the Stephanus references alone.

PREFACE

This little book began in some lectures on the *Utopia* which I was giving to first-year students in the Foundation Year Programme at the University of King's College. The programme had been started as an alternative to the ordinary unstructured selection of five first-year courses which became the norm after North American universities had generally abandoned the curriculum in the late 1960s. This four-credit course sought to provide a coherent account of the development of Western civilization from Homer to the twentieth century. By late November, when I was to lecture on More, I had either taught, or tutored and sat through, a series of classes on Homer, Sophocles, the *Republic*, the *Aeneid*, some of Augustine, the *Song of Roland* and all three parts of the *Divine Comedy*. In preparing my lecture I happened to look up a note in the text we were using (Paul Turner's translation in the Penguin edition) on More's use of the title "Bencheater" for the second highest set of officials in Utopia. This appeared to be one of the many names he had concocted from Greek roots.[1] I found the following explanation:

> BENCHEATER: *Traniborus*, possibly from *thranos* (bench) and *bora* (food). If so, the name may have been suggested by memories of Lincoln's Inn, where More's grandfather and father had both held the post of butler, and he himself had been a Reader; where communal meals were eaten by members sitting on benches; and where Senior Members were known as Benchers. (Glossary, p. 153)

Further research revealed more in the same vein (see for example the note in the Yale ed., p. 398, 122/10-13), but the explanation seemed lame. In the case of all the other made-up names, More did so because their objects were fictional: thus Anemolius, Utopia, the Polylerites, Achorians, Macarians, Amaurotum, Abraxa, Anydrus, etc. When he

Reference notes to the Preface appear on pp. xi-xiii.

refers to real places or characters he uses their proper names—as in Antwerp, England, France, Plato and Aristotle. Why would he make up a name to refer to a real situation in this case and, if it did refer to the Benchers of Lincoln's Inn, what would this have to do with his argument? Likewise, in our text, the lower officials were called "Stywards"—with the following note:

> STYWARD: *Syphograntus*, possibly from *suephos* (pig-sty) and *krantor* (ruler). Like *Traniborus*, this name may have some connexion with Lincoln's Inn, where More's grandfather was not only butler but also steward (which was sometimes spelt *styward*). (Glossary, p. 154)

Only a month earlier I had been discussing with students the difficult questions about the beginning of Book II of the *Republic* and, perhaps because I had also been considering the development of Western thought from Plato to More in the intervening period, I suddenly thought I saw what More intended. These terms had nothing to do with Lincoln's Inn! Rather, they were intended as a playful reference, for his learned humanist readers, to Plato's *Republic*.[2] There, in Book II, where Socrates begins by constructing a state in thought, he first gives us what he calls the "true ... healthy state" (372e). This is a simple Arcadian paradise that aims at nothing beyond the bare necessities of food, clothing and shelter (see 369a-372d) sought in a rational manner in a settled agricultural community. Glaucon, his interlocutor, spurns this rustic simplicity in these words:

> ... if you were founding a city of pigs, Socrates, what other fodder than this would you provide?
>
> Why, what would you have, Glaucon? said I [Socrates].
>
> What is customary, he replied. They must recline on couches, I presume, if they are not to be uncomfortable, and dine from tables and have dishes and sweetmeats such as are now in use. (372d-e)

From this point on Socrates turns his attention, through the rest of the *Republic*, to the demands of the "luxurious city" (372e) that can provide for such refined wants. He never returns to the Arcadian paradise. For Plato it was lost beyond recovery in the simpler and purer past of man's original innocence. But was not this "city of pigs" what More was referring to in the titles he playfully invented for the officials of Utopia? If the correct derivation of syphogrant was "the ruler of a pig-sty"—as seemed beyond dispute if only some plausible meaning could be attached to it—perhaps this was the sense More intended: i.e., that he conceived of Utopia as a kind of realization of the Arcadian state that Plato had thought of as the true and healthy one but which he had had to abandon in his concern to cope with the luxurious desires of men. If this was the case, it was a perfect piece of Moronic humour to imply that the basic administrative unit of the Utopian version of Plato's Arcadian paradise (= Glaucon's "city of pigs") was a sty—thirty families ruled by a sty-ward or syphogrant (123/11)!

This interpretation gained plausibility through a similar consideration of the other Greek title of the higher officials, the tranibors, who ruled "over ten syphogrants with their families" (123/10). In Glaucon's reply to Socrates the very first thing which he mentions to distinguish the "customary" desires of men (i.e., their ordinary, but corrupt, expectations) from the strict necessities of the Arcadian city was the provision of the usual couches and tables for eating. In Arcadia these luxuries were not provided and the citizens ate from the ground, "reclined on rustic beds (στιβάς = a bed of straw, rushes or leaves) strewed with bryony and myrtle" (372b). Against this Glaucon insists that if Socrates' city is to have any relevance to the real life of the Greeks, then its citizens "must recline on couches (κλίνη)... and dine from tables" (372d). Since the habit of eating in the reclining position had long passed, More, with as much humour as accuracy, chose not to call the higher officials klinobors, for "Coucheaters," but tranibors, or "Bencheaters." And, by the same token as above, this carried with it the suggestion that, in the whole Utopian state, these few elected officials alone—the syphogrants, tranibors, and the governor, or *Princeps*, of each town (123/16)[3]—must be thought to stand in some way outside of Plato's Arcadia since, by the name "Bencheater," they are identified with that activity which first led Plato beyond the Arcadian city. On closer inspection it appeared that the reason More gave this name was to stress that the presence of these offices constituted the fundamental difference between Utopia and the Platonic Arcadia[4]—made necessary by More's desire to describe in detail the requirements for establishing a true and healthy state like the Arcadian paradise which Plato dreamed of but was unable to realize. All of this seemed to fit very well with the lines More himself wrote and prefaced to his work in the *Hexastichon*:

> Plato's Republic now I claim
> To match, or beat at its own game
> For that was just a myth in prose
> But what he wrote of I became
> Eutopia is now my name.
>
> (tr. Turner)

From this starting point I began to consider whether the connection between *Utopia* and the *Republic* might not be a good deal more pervasive and profound than was revealed in the literature and, if so, what it might mean. This study of the first book of the *Utopia* contains the result of these reflections and while, in one sense, its aim is strictly limited to a commentary on Book I the reader will find that this is treated in the broadest context.

More (1478-1535) stands at the beginnings of modern political thought and I will argue that he grasped all the essential features of the modern state. But what makes his work especially interesting and useful is that he—more clearly than either his contemporary Machiavelli (1469-1527) or that other great fountainhead of modern politics, Thomas Hobbes (1588-1679)—presents the modern position quite self-consciously and explicitly in its distinction from the failed political order of the Middle Ages on the one hand and from the surpassed position of the ancients on the other. For this reason my ostensibly narrow study ranges broadly and I have found it necessary to speak about the political order of both medieval Christendom and antiquity—and to distinguish in the latter between the political theory which Plato developed in Greece and the practical politics of the Romans. The reader should be aware of two special problems in my book. They come from a rather sharp difference between what I say and some widely held views about what Plato taught on the one hand and what the modern political theory that began with Machiavelli, More and Hobbes was all about on the other. In relation to the first I find myself in a rather uncomfortable bind because my argument does switch back and forth between the *Utopia* and the *Republic*. Scholars and students alike will perhaps wonder about the interpretation of the *Republic* which they will find here, so much at odds with a great deal of contemporary opinion on the purpose and meaning of Plato's doctrine. I ask these readers to bear in mind that this book is not itself a commentary on the *Republic* and I claim only that, in general, the interpretation of Plato presented here is the one which was held by *More* (and his humanist friends). The other problem, which again is not directly related to the thesis of the book, concerns the strongly negative judgement of Leo Strauss on Machiavelli, Hobbes and, by implication, More. Here too, while I do not want to pick an argument with Strauss, his views are so widely held and so influential that I have thought it important to state where the things we shall discover about More suggest the necessity of some modification in the Straussian position. For the most part I have confined the discussion of these two matters to the footnotes. In my view the *Utopia* allows us, or rather forces us, as does no other work, to see and understand the development of the modern political order in the context of the entire Western tradition, and on this account above all others I think it is a singular and invaluable gift from More to us. He can show us where we are and where we are going because he knows where we have been.

As this book both began, and was nurtured, through my contact with the lecturers, tutors and students of the Foundation Year Programme, I would like to express my debt to that remarkable group—who have all contributed in one way or another—and gratefully dedicate it to the Foundation Year Programme with special thanks for the careful reading and helpful suggestions of my colleagues R. D. Crouse, W. J. Hankey and K. Kierans. Thanks also to Olive Koyama and the staff at Wilfrid Laurier University Press and especially to its Director, Sandra

Woolfrey, for the fairness, understanding and decency she has shown me throughout.

This book has been published with the help of a grant from the Canadian Federation for the Humanities, using funds provided by the Social Sciences and Humanities Research Council of Canada.

University of King's College   C. S.
Halifax, Nova Scotia
May 1988

Notes to the Preface

1   The Yale ed. (p. 398, 122/10-13) notes that G. J. Vossius, in his edition of More's works (*Opera*, Vol. 4, p. 340, Amsterdam, 1695-1701), "refuses to concern himself with *Syphograntus* and *Traniborus* relying on More's denial that they are based on the Greek." Surtz, however, goes on to give various possible Greek roots—referring to the derivations of Lupton (ed. *Utopia*, London and Paris, 1777), in addition to the possibilities he himself suggests. The Greek origin of these words is obvious and More's playful denial comes from the distinction between the older forms of these titles which were used before the Utopians (re)learned Greek from Raphael, and the newer, consciously Greek forms: see below, n. 2. Raphael tells us how we are to understand the matter at 181/25-30 where he says, "According to my conjecture, they got hold of Greek literature more easily because it was somewhat related to their own. I suspect that their race was derived from the Greek because their language, which in almost all other respects resembles the Persian, retains some traces of Greek in the names of their cities *and officials*" (emphasis mine).

2   On More's intended audience, see the first section of the Introduction. As corroboration of the argument that More had a double audience in mind—i.e., the new Renaissance Humanists who could be supposed to have a good knowledge of Plato, and another group, equally learned but educated in the old scholastic manner, who could not—we should note that along with the "ancient" (*prisca lingua*, 122/10) forms of *syphogrant* and *tranibor*, the meaning of which, as I interpret them, could only make sense to one who knew the *Republic* well, More also provides the "newer" (*recentiore*, 122/10) Utopian synonyms of *phylarch* and *protophylarch* ("head of a tribe" and "first among chieftains"—Yale ed., p. 398, 122/10-13). The sense of these latter words would be clear to anyone who knew Greek even if they were unfamiliar with Plato. Apart from such a double audience it is hard to see why More would have bothered with the double forms.

3   More refers to the highest officials in Utopia—the heads of each of the fifty-four cities—by the Latin word *princeps*, "governor" (122/15). Several pages later, and evidently as an afterthought because they are not mentioned where the other Utopian forms are given, he tells us the Utopian names of the *princeps*: *Barzanes* in the older tongue, and *Ademus* in the newer (see 133/5-9). The latter, as the Yale ed. notes (p. 411, 132/8), "is evidently formed from ἁ-privative and δῆμος, 'people,' and therefore means 'Peopleless.'" This would be clear to anyone who read Greek and is probably intended to carry the sense that these "rulers" have no subjects in the conventional, or Platonic, sense (see below, n. 4). *Barzanes* is more difficult to interpret although I set aside the suggestion(?) in the Yale ed. (*ibid.*) that it may come from the name of some actual

person or character such as the *Mithrobarzanes* mentioned in Lucian's *Menippus*—which, along with other of his satires, More had translated with Erasmus (on these translations, see the works cited in the Yale ed., p. clxii, n. 1). If this is what More is supposed to have done here it would run counter to all the other Utopian names which he himself concocted—and we will be faced with a number of other possibilities with no definite means of choosing between them, such as the following suggested to me by R. D. Crouse: (i) *Bardesanes*, a Syrian Christian who became a sort of Gnostic skilled in philosophy and who wrote a treatise on the Laws of Countries, directed towards Marcus Aurelius, showing how the *mores* of peoples vary, not according to fate, but free will; (ii) the *Bardesanians*, a fifth-century Egyptian monophysite sect; (iii) *Barsanuphius*, the notorious sixth-century Palestinian hermit. All these names would have been known in More's time, from Augustine, Eusebius, John of Damascus, etc.

I think a better interpretative principle is to suppose that More intended to help his readers, within the limits allowed by the form he had chosen, and so was consistent in making up all the Utopian names. I thus find much more likely the suggestion of the Yale ed. (*ibid.*) that *barzanes* comes from the Hebrew *bar*, "בר‎", 'son of' and Ζάνος, Doric poetic form of the genitive of Zeus." In this case More would be giving, as the title of the highest Utopian officials, a form of the epithet "son of Zeus," which the Greeks gave to their greatest heroes and true rulers from Achilles to Alexander the Great. The difficulty here is that the Hebrew component does not accord with Raphael's explicit hint (text quoted above, n. 1) that the old Utopian names of the officials are related to Greek—even though More would, of course have been familiar with the Hebrew *bar* from the Greek Bible. If, as I think, the word should be derived from Greek alone, the root βάρ—as in βάρβαρος—conveys the sense of "bleating" or "talking foolishly" (see the etymology of *balo* in Lewis and Short, *A Latin Dictionary*, Oxford, Clarendon Press, 1969), and so the whole would mean something like "the one who babbles of God" or "the foolish one of God." I understand *barzanes* in this sense as specifying that—unlike the traditional or Platonic view of the ruler who, from More's point of view, was falsely presumed to know the divine will for all earthly things—the highest officials in the true commonwealth are those who "babbled of God" rather than pretending to have a knowledge which allowed them to speak definitely about those things which were inscrutable to them. This is simply another form of the same idea that More conveys in Raphael's name (see below, p. 24). The one gives the characteristic of a true "ruler" who does not presume to judge and speak with the mind of God, the other gives the characteristic of a true "philosopher" who knows nonsense when he hears it and knows that he knows nothing else. These amount to the same thing from the side of both action and knowledge since the true ruler and the true philosopher stand closest to God in their common knowledge that, in respect to wisdom, they are really worthless.

4 Plato mentions no laws and no rulers whatsoever in Arcadia (see *Republic*, 369a-372d). A close examination of the "rulers" in Utopia lies beyond the scope of this essay—because it really belongs to Book II—but the following remarks may be helpful. More, the character, notices this point from the first time Raphael mentions the Utopian communism. More maintains that if all people are really equal then no one would have authority over any other nor would there be respect for any office—with the consequence that nobody would pay any attention to the laws (see 107/10-16). In Book II Raphael tells how this is not so in Utopia. He says, "No official is haughty or formidable. They are called fathers and show that character. Honor is paid them willingly, as it should be, and is not extracted from the reluctant" (195/1-4). From the standpoint of Antiquity and the Middle Ages it is not possible to have laws without real rulers to enforce them—because the law, coming from the intelligible and divine realm, is opposed to the immediate desires of men and women and must therefore be imposed on them by powerful rulers. Although the Utopians are ruled by law, there is no single ruler

of the whole republic. Each of the fifty-four cities has its syphogrants, tranibors and a governor: there is also a national senate (see 113/26-29 and 147/33-34). Anarchy is not the result because the law in Utopia is understood to be already present (by divine institution) in man's nature, and so to live virtuously one has only to live according to nature (see 163/22-26). Since the law is thought to be within each person there is no necessity for a ruler to bring it down from on high and enforce it from without. Each one possesses it as much as any other. The only function of the rulers is therefore a kind of gentle, paternal urging to remind people to look within themselves to find their own best interests and this too is the function of the law (see 195/8-39). Occasionally they must act decisively, with capital punishment, when through some defect in the nature of an individual the body politic is threatened (see 191/34-36), but for the most part they are simply the most convenient means of organizing the uniform distribution of the common commodities (see 147/33-149/4). Being no "closer" to the law than any other person they do not rule by any special divine status or right of birth. They must therefore be elected (see 123/8-23) and their position is an office in the modern sense—i.e., one that anyone can hold, whose nature and training makes suited to the task (see 133/5-9 where the ambassadors, priests, tranibors and governors are chosen from the educated—*ex ordine literatorum*—but only because the job requires these skills). In all these particulars More had arrived at a truly modern conception of law and rule.

A close analogy in More's own day is found—in relation to the reform of the church rather than the state—in Luther's doctrine of the priesthood of all believers with the consequent reduction of the sacerdotal status of priests to an office (of ministry) at the pleasure of the people and solely for the convenience of organization.

In the *Babylonian Captivity of the Church* (1520), Luther writes words that precisely echo More's—although More came to be opposed to Luther for doing to the church the very same thing that he (More) had done to the state. Luther says, "If they [his Catholic opponents] were forced to grant that all of us that have been baptized are equally priests, as indeed we are, and that only the ministry was committed to them, yet with our common consent, they would then know that they have no right to rule over us except insofar as we freely concede it" (in *Three Treatises, Martin Luther*, from the American Edition of *Luther's Works*, Vol. 36, trans. A. T. W. Steinhäuser, rev. Frederick C. Ahrens and Abdel Ross Wentz, Philadelphia, Fortress Press, 1960, pp. 244-45). Luther's tone and even, frequently, his images—i.e., shepherds turned into wolves (*ibid.*, p. 244; compare *Utopia*, 65/10)—are the same as More's.

INTRODUCTION

More's *Utopia* is a very strange book for the twentieth-century reader. Although it is short, clear, vivacious and easily read, one finishes, on the first or the tenth attempt, with the feeling that the work has somehow disintegrated in the reading. It is like one of those wooden puzzles, a segmented ball, where we seem always to end with some dominant idea that approximates the whole and yet find ourselves left with a number of awkward-shaped pieces that cannot be made to fit. H. G. Wells expressed this commonly felt difficulty when he wrote that *Utopia* was "one of the most profoundly inconsistent of books" in its mixing of what seem like irreconcilable ideas[1]—and this characteristic, felt by every student, accounts for the many conflicting interpretations which have been produced in this century. By some the work is seen as a simple *jeu d'esprit*, a "holiday work," of no serious consequence,[2] and by others as a most profound piece of political philosophy;[3] to some it is the expression of the strictest medieval Catholicism,[4] and to others of the most atheistic communism.[5]

The variety and mutual exclusiveness of these views leaves us in a difficult position. It will readily be allowed that each account looks like the original in some ways and yet, because they are contradictory insofar as each presents itself as the true account of the whole, it appears impossible to hold together all the parts of the original. It seems that contemporary interpreters have either been content to look to a description of some part of what More says without attempting to put the whole together, or else, fitting together such pieces as they can, have been forced to the unhappy expedient of reconstituting the ball by sanding off the protruding pieces and filling in the gaps with sawdust.

Throughout this essay I assume that More had some definite thing he wanted to say and that he said it in the best and most intelligible way he

Reference notes to the Introduction appear on pp. 11-17.

knew how—given what he knew of the audience to whom he was speaking. This is what I would like to uncover—working from the assumption that it is there to be found. In other words, I do not *want* to have to accept Wells' conclusion that More wrote and published a work which he knew to be "profoundly inconsistent."[6] But this is not to deny that, from our standpoint, many apparent inconsistencies have allowed the mutually contradictory interpretations of our own day. How are we to explain this? If we suppose that More himself was neither inconsistent nor incompetent, how is it that we see many inconsistencies when the book itself has not changed? We may suspect that our difficulties, in arriving at an understanding of the work as a coherent whole, arise primarily from the many differences, in prejudice and point of view, between ourselves and the sixteenth century. In other words what we seem to lack is a share in the principle More had in mind in composing the *Utopia*—and we will have this, and can know we have it, only if we can read and understand the book without altering any piece and with none left over.

Where should we look to find such a principle? I suggest that the answer must lie in something both More and his intended audience possessed in common; otherwise we would have to suppose that he wrote a book which none of his contemporaries could have understood. That More and some, at any rate, of his readers shared such a principle can be deduced from those sixteenth-century figures whose opinions we know—his humanist friends and admirers[7]—all of whom are unanimous in praise of the book and who are all agreed that its meaning is clear and unambiguous.[8] The conflicting interpretations of the twentieth century have no parallel in the sixteenth and this itself deserves our attention.

If we look to the evidence of More's contemporaries it is impossible to argue, as does Kautsky, that More was "a whole epoch in advance of his time," having perceived "a newly evolving mode of production and its social consequences not only sooner than most of his contemporaries, but straining far into the future, also glimpse[d] the more rational mode of production into which it will develop" (*Thomas More and His Utopia*, p. 161).

If, as Kautsky would have it, a unique set of circumstances impelled More, "alone in his age," to make the "bold intellectual leap" to modern Socialism, then it will follow, as he maintains, that "The drift of his speculation, of course, escaped his contemporaries and can only be appreciated by us today" (p. 161). This does not accord with the evidence. The testimony of his contemporaries is unanimous: they thought they understood the *Utopia* very well. But perhaps they were all mistaken as to More's real intentions? In this case More should either have objected to their interpretation, or else he could not have been the Socialist Kautsky claims he was. More did not make any such objection.

Rather, he was delighted with the opinions and commendations as we can readily see from their publication with his text.

We have decided to begin looking for the principle we seek in something shared by More and his intended audience. We will be greatly helped if we can specify the latter. Fortunately this is now established beyond all reasonable doubt. The central tradition of recent interpretation finds that More belonged to, and in the first instance wrote the *Utopia* for, an audience of Northern Renaissance Humanists. A great body of scholarship develops this thesis, enumerates the circle of More's friends and acquaintances,[9] and discusses the religious, political, social, economic and intellectual concerns of these men.[10] It is no part of my intention to recapitulate this work except as it touches directly on the thesis of this essay, yet I am indebted to the findings of these scholars and take for granted their general conclusion as stated above.

In one respect especially the analogy of a puzzle is particularly well suited to the *Utopia* since it is a "designedly enigmatic book."[11] In an obvious sense More composed it as a kind of literary puzzle by blending real and imaginary characters, places and times with the aim of establishing the gentle fiction that Utopia was contiguous in time and space with sixteenth-century Europe. This is a fiction in which the early commentators were delighted to join. But more than this, and at quite another level, More published the work with a number of enigmatic references which explicitly or implicitly invite the reader to compare it with, above all else, Plato's *Republic*. This process begins with the very title which is not simply *Utopia* but *De optimo REIPUBLICAE statu deque nova insula Utopia* (emphasis mine).[12] Such an invitation could only be taken up by those readers who had a close acquaintance with Plato's work and these constituted the audience More had directly in mind in writing the book. But this does not mean that it was directed at them exclusively.

The thesis of this essay is that More composed the *Utopia* as a rewriting of Plato's *Republic* in which he answered its central question in a form that would be relevant to his own day. The *Utopia* is the *Republic* recast in a new mould applicable to the demands of contemporary Christianity as these were understood by More and his circle of reforming friends. In a word, it is a Christianized *Republic*.

This premise immediately calls for some modification of what we have just said about the intended reader. In part this audience was certainly that group of Northern Renaissance Humanists who shared the methods, aims and interests of Erasmus. Such men are represented by those who contributed to the early editions: Thierry Martens, John Froben, Jerome Busleyden, Peter Giles, Gerhard Geldenhauer, Thomas Lupset, William Budé, Beatus Rhenanus, John Desmarais, Cornelius de Schrijver, Willibald Pirckheimer and, above all, Erasmus himself.[13] But More also intended the work for the much wider audience of all educated persons who could read Latin.[14] He was not mistaken about their interest, as we may judge from the many editions the Latin text went through in the century following its first publication and before it had time to prove itself or be purchased as a classic. This general audience was soon broadened further by the publication of the first English translation—by Ralph Robinson, in 1551—sixteen years after More's execution.[15] I understand this long initial popularity as an indication that, beyond any vogue, it spoke in a significant manner to questions of the day which were seen as both important and interesting.[16]

Though it seems obvious, the specification of this double audience is important since it clarifies an aspect of the work that has tended to mislead modern interpreters and it removes an improbable conclusion to which recent studies have tended. On the first point, while scholars have often recognized More's pre-eminent debt to Plato, this has for the most part been treated in a very external manner by the simple cataloguing of similarities and differences.[17] There are two reasons for this. On the one hand the most peremptory references, which invite the broadest comparison with the *Republic*, are not found in the text itself but are contained in the prefatory materials: the *Tetrastichon*, *Hexastichon*, and the letters from Giles to Busleyden, Busleyden to More, and Rhenanus to Pirckheimer. All of these, with the exception of the *Hexastichon* or "Six lines on the island of Utopia by Anemolius," were written by persons other than More.[18] This has tended to blunt their force. It is generally assumed that since he did not compose them they are not his views and need not be seriously considered for the interpretation of the work. The second reason is that while Plato is mentioned more frequently than any other author, there are still no more than half a dozen explicit references in the text itself and many of these are incidental.[19] When placed against the host of other authors, pagan, patristic, medieval and contemporary whom More is known to have read and whose works have evident parallels to parts of the *Utopia*,[20] the central position which I claim for the *Republic* has been obscured.

If More intended the *Utopia* to be seen as a Christianized *Republic* then we must consider why he so limited the explicit references to Plato that the relationship becomes enigmatic. The answer lies in the double audience for whom he was writing. Partly this consisted of those trained and educated in the new learning who knew the *Republic* well and who, with the gentlest of reminders, would easily see and delight in the many subtle references he makes throughout the book. For such men the profound relation to the *Republic* was obvious and the explicit references almost too loud. On the other hand, as he was also writing for a much wider audience who would not know the *Republic* as did the first group, or even at all, he had to take care not to make his message dependent on an understanding which they neither had nor could easily get.

This was not a problem since More was confident that the essentials of the Platonic doctrine were so embedded in contemporary attitudes and institutions—i.e., in the Platonic positions he criticizes in Book I—that he would have no difficulty in describing them in forms that every reader could recognize. There was thus no need to begin by bringing such readers to an explicit knowledge of the *Republic*.

More may well have borrowed this technique for speaking to two audiences (one more educated and the other less) from his favourite, Augustine, who does the same thing in his *Confessions*. At the crucial point where Augustine tells how, after fourteen years of searching, he came to the true idea of God, he says that he was guided to this knowledge by reading "certain books of the Platonists" (VII,ix,13). Though he could easily have done so, he refuses to identify the books in question and instead paraphrases their content in words drawn exclusively from the New Testament. This is very frustrating for modern scholars who would love to know which books of what "Platonist" authors he read (Plato? Plotinus? Porphyry?)—but Augustine's reasons for this intentional obscurity are clear. Those who knew the Platonist idea of God did not need to be told what it was. They would have no trouble recognizing it. On the other hand he affirms that those who did not have any philosophical training need not try to acquire it by reading the Platonists, because the same truth which was found in their works was also contained in the Christian position of the ordinary reader—along with a further truth which was not: i.e., that the eternal and incorporeal God whom both Platonists and Christians recognized in common had also become man (see VII,ix,13-15).[21] In other words, Augustine is saying to the simple Christian reader who lacks philosophical culture: "Look, I first found the true idea of God in the books of the Platonists—but you don't have to bother to study them because, as I later discovered, the very same idea of God is also found in the Scriptures which you know and possess." More's intent is similar, except that in his case the Platonic teachings he is concerned with are those dealing with the state.

The explicit recognition of this wider audience saves us also from an improbable result which has appeared in the works of recent humanist interpreters. On the whole this school proceeds by the careful and diligent study of the sources—chiefly classical—which More is thought to have used. But with each advance in the complexity and sophistication of interpretation the group of readers More could have been addressing becomes smaller and smaller since it appears that they would have had to know more and more in order to understand his real purpose. The end result, in a recent and otherwise excellent book (Logan's *Meaning*), is the conclusion that "*Utopia* has proved to be too sophisticated for its readers, both in substance and in literary method" (p. 3). Although Logan's work is poles apart from what he justly calls "the ideological special pleading and appalling anachronism" (p. 7) of Kautsky, he nevertheless ends up in the same position on this question: i.e., that More wrote a book which few or none in his day could possibly have understood. Without disputing any of the particular findings of these scholars, this conclusion, in and of itself, is so unlikely that some revision of any thesis that ends up in this position is surely necessary.[22] However restricted one part of More's audience might have been, the work must be so understood that it could also have been accessible to a wider audience. Otherwise we will be forced to maintain that the tremendous popularity of *Utopia* in More's own day, and in the century following its publication, was based on a complete misapprehension of his real intent by the majority of his readers—or else we must deny his evident care and success in writing in a simple, witty and widely appealing fashion as if the work was merely a specialized technical treatise.[23]

More himself called his work, *On the best kind of a Republic and about the new island of Utopia*. This title gives the topic, or rather the topics, which correspond to the two books of the text. The first part of the title, "About the best kind of a Republic," would immediately suggest to his learned readers that More was going to criticize Plato who, while he had given us the first Republic, has not apparently given us the *best*. The second book, on Utopia, building on the criticisms of Plato in the first, uses them to alter those positions from Plato's *Republic* which need amendment and presents us with the true commonwealth.

This interpretation appears to run afoul of J. H. Hexter's important findings about the order in which More composed the *Utopia*.[24] Erasmus remarks, in his letter to Ulrich von Hutten (23 July 1517), that More "had written the second book at his leisure, and afterwards, when he found it was required, added the first offhand. Hence there is some inequality in the style."[25] From this evidence Hexter proceeded to ask what, precisely, the latter-written segment included, given cogent reasons why it could not simply be Book I. In general his answer is that More wrote the introduction and the discourse on Utopia (Book II) in Antwerp and then later added some prefatory lines, the entire dialogue of Book I on the conditions in England, and a few concluding pages. It is not necessary for me to recapitulate or criticize his findings in detail. This has been ably done by Logan who argues against Hexter's "thoroughly disintegrative reading" (*Meaning*, p. 15),[26] which came from his consideration that the work was written under two different impulses and which resulted in his conclusion that "the published version of *Utopia* falls into two parts which represent two different and separate sets of intention on the part of the author."[27]

Against this, Logan insists that we must "take as our working assumption that More knew what he was doing and if he reopened a completed book he did so to make it better, not to conflate it with a different one" (pp. 16-17). Logan therefore concludes (p. 18) that it seems "likely that examining the sections of *Utopia* consecutively—that is, in the order in which More meant them to be read—is the best critical procedure," and in this I agree with him.

What remains for us to explain is why More would have written the second book first—Hythloday's Discourse on Utopia—as a Christian correction of Plato and then, later, have written most of the first book in which he developed the criticism of Plato which had informed the basis of his earlier correction. This appears to be putting the cart before the horse.

As a starting point let us consider the immediate circumstances surrounding the composition of the Discourse on Utopia (i.e., Book II). I think the most likely account is that given by Hexter (Yale ed., pp. xxvii-xxxiii) of the conversations More and Peter Giles probably had in Antwerp in the summer of 1515 as they were in the process of becoming friends. The general question of how best to order a commonwealth was clearly on the minds of many of Europe's most thoughtful men at the time—and it was there because it was pressing.[28] The older medieval view of a unified Christendom with the Emperor as its temporal head and the Pope as the spiritual leader had everywhere broken down—chiefly through the Investiture Controversy—in the inability of these two powers to agree on a limit to their respective spheres and competing claims of supremacy.[29] Pope after pope claimed supremacy over the temporal rulers while these, in turn, claimed their independence from the Pope. The result was that the political structure which had informed Europe for a millennium was collapsing into chaos on all sides. This process had been going on for a very long time and by More's day it had become clear to the best minds that there was no hope of patching up or restoring the old system.

Already two centuries earlier, Dante had despaired of any resolution. We can see this in the unresolved conflict between the "harlot" (*una puttana* = the Church) and the "giant" (*un gigante* = the Empire) in the Beatrician pageant of Church and State which unfolds in the Earthly Paradise (*Purgatorio* Cto. XXXII, 148-60). Nothing in the intervening period had worked to restore the balanced relation of these two—on which not only medieval political theory but also the whole medieval era itself had depended.[30] On the side of the spiritual claims of the temporal rulers, More, in his lifetime, was to see his own king break England from the spiritual leadership of the Pope and appoint himself to that position in his stead. On the other side, the unremitting worldliness of the popes (Sixtus IV, Innocent VIII, Alexander VI and Julius II)—to speak only of the ones who held the chair during More's lifetime prior to writing the *Utopia*—was notorious throughout the Christian world. During the first half of the sixteenth century when the consequences of this confusion were evident everywhere, always, and to all, thoughtful men in Europe were forced to turn their attention to the desperate political problem which resulted from the collapse of the medieval system.

They reacted in a variety of ways. For the sake of contrast it will be useful to consider briefly the other, equally famous, response to the political question in Niccolo Machiavelli's *Prince*. This was written at almost the same time (1513) as More's *Utopia* (1515), though neither man had any knowledge of the other. In Machiavelli's Italy the vacuum created by the final collapse of the medieval political order[31] had left a problem which, above all else, cried out for a strong man to impose a practical solution. This is just what Machiavelli was hoping to promote through his work—as he makes clear in the final chapter of the *Prince*. In England however—where there was no vacuum in political matters since Henry VIII was nothing if not a strong king—these problems presented themselves in a slightly different form. For More the question was what would be the best political system to replace the order that had informed Europe since Ambrose and Augustine, in the fourth century, had first defined the balance of powers.[32]

Considerations of this kind were, in all likelihood, the tenor of the conversations More had with Peter Giles in Antwerp in 1515.[33] Their answers became the substance of the description of Utopia (i.e., Book II). For their point of departure they took Plato's *Republic* as *the* classic treatise on this question and then began to alter and modify its teachings as they deemed necessary to make it answerable to contemporary Europe. We can be reasonably certain of this—if it is right to pretend to any certainty about the private conversation of two men over 450 years ago—from the fact that all of Giles' contributions to the text of *Utopia* remark pointedly on its relation to the *Republic*,[34] and because More accepts them without surprise or qualification. Giles' insistence and More's silence are difficult to explain if this identification had not been at the very centre of their talk.

The choice of the *Republic* as the classic treatise on how best to order a commonwealth deserves some comment. The first question is why More and Giles thought it proper to reach back to antiquity for the basic text which anyone addressing this question would have to consider. We have already given the answer. None of the political writings of the patristic or medieval period would do as the starting point of the inquiry. What had become clear all over Europe was that no amount of tinkering with the older system could make it work and, further, that all appeals to either prince or prelate, urging them to limit their ambition, fell on deaf ears. The time-honoured form of these appeals was the *speculum prin-*

cipis, such as Erasmus' *The Education of a Christian Prince*—a mirror held up to princes by the learned to induce them to improve their behaviour. By More's day these amounted to nothing more than what Hexter has correctly characterized as "futile moral incantation."[35] To find a starting point which was not involved in the problem it was necessary to go back beyond any position which assumed the older Christian view of the separation and relation of the two powers—and More and Giles went to Plato.

Next we must ask why they settled on Plato's *Republic* rather than any of the other ancient texts which were equally well known, such as Isocrates' *To Nicocles*, Xenophon's *Cyropaedia*, Aristotle's *Politics* or, on the Roman side, the political works of Cicero or to Vergil's *Aeneid*.[36] The answer here lies in part with the general enthusiasm of the Renaissance Humanists for the newly rediscovered Platonic *Dialogues*, translated and published (1483-84) by Marsilio Ficino and promoted in the Platonic Academy he started at Florence. More certainly knew of this work through John Colet, the dean of St. Paul's in London, who was greatly influenced by Ficino.[37] More's interest in Plato, prior to writing the *Utopia*, is well attested. He had already translated into English the biography of Pico della Mirandola, one of the most famous members of the Florentine school. Further, Erasmus wrote to von Hutten that, "while still a youth, he [More] attempted a dialogue, in which he carried the defence of Plato's community even to the matter of wives!"[38] This shows also that More had read the *Republic* from his youth—a point echoed by his biographer, Stapleton, who also says that More "read especially Plato and his followers . . . because he considered their teaching most useful in the government of the state and the preservation of civic order."[39]

The second reason for selecting the *Republic* lies, I think, in Augustine's praise of Plato as the epitome of natural reason. For Augustine, Plato had been *the* philosopher of antiquity who had best expressed those truths which man can attain to on his own. In the *City of God* he develops this position explicitly and at length.[40] Augustine teaches that the wise men of all nations, insofar as they spoke the truth, said only what Plato had first said more fully and more clearly.[41] One should therefore turn to Plato to find such truths as man can know apart from the Christian religion or, to put the same thing in another way, to find those truths which the Christian religion shares with all mankind. In the same letter to von Hutten, Erasmus tells us that, again when More was "scarcely more than a youth," he had "lectured publicly on the *De Civitate Dei* of Augustine before a numerous audience, old men and priests not being ashamed to take a lesson in divinity from a young layman, and not at all sorry to have done so."[42] In More's eyes, strongly influenced as he was by Augustine, Plato was thus the first and finest authority to consult on the question of the best-ordered commonwealth if one wanted to know what truths man could come to by reason alone.[43]

But More's audience, whether taken in the narrow or the broad sense, was thoroughly Christian. His readers were all inheritors of a millennium and a half of the Christianization of European thought, perceptions, aspirations and institutions. For both More and Giles this meant that the doctrines of the *Republic* could have no immediate application. What was needed was a revision of the *Republic* in the light of contemporary Christianity which would distinguish between what was acceptable in Plato's work and what was not—and which could do both of these things without in any way falling back on the other, now failed, answer that the West had first given to the political question at the beginning of the medieval era. This is what More set out to accomplish in his *Utopia*.

There is one final matter we should deal with before turning to the work itself. This concerns the different content of Books I and II. Hexter's discovery of a compositional seam near the beginning of Book I led him to postulate different impulsions under which More wrote Book II first, in Flanders, and then Book I, in London, on his return. In Hexter's account, the main content of Book I—about how and whether a philosopher should serve a prince—came directly out of More's reflections on the freshly written Discourse on Utopia when he considered this in the light of the offer of a place at court, made to him by Henry VIII and Wolsey soon after he got back to England.[44] I do not object to Hexter's well-founded observations on this matter except for what he has to say about how More saw the connection between the later-written Book I and the earlier-written Book II. In the Yale edition Hexter "downplays the theme of disunity" from his earlier position[45] by recognizing that "those points of view, opinions, modes of thinking and feeling that occur in both the Discourse and the Dialogue cannot be dismissed as passing fancies or ill-considered trifles."[46] But even so, he is still forced by his two-impulsion theory to leave disintegrated all those sections of the Discourse of Book II which find no parallel in the Dialogue of Book I;[47] and he can say nothing very definite about the relation of the first- to the second-written parts except as the latter echo the former.

I believe we can do much more. My thesis is that Book II embodies the conversations of More and Giles in which they "rewrote," with playful tone but serious intent, those aspects of the *Republic* which were applicable to their world. The substance of Book I which More wrote later, no doubt as an afterthought,[48] and very likely under the influences suggested by Hexter, nevertheless belongs *logically* to the Discourse. In it More developed the criticism of those teachings in the *Republic* which he and Giles had not accepted because they were part and parcel of the contemporary problem. Book I therefore provides the reader with an explicit basis for understanding the superiority of Utopia both to the unacceptable parts of the Platonic Republic and to such elements in the contemporary European scene as were images of those elements. In short, Book I shows the Christian criticism of the *Republic* while Book II shows the sixteenth century what it could and should take from it.

Notes to the Introduction

1 See H. G. Wells, "Introduction," in *Utopia*, Limited Editions Club, New York, Heritage Press, 1935.

2 C. S. Lewis (*English Literature in the Sixteenth Century, Excluding Drama*, The Oxford History of English Literature, Vol. 3, Oxford, Clarendon Press, 1954) writes of *Utopia* that "It becomes intelligible and delightful as soon as we take it for what it is—a holiday work, a spontaneous overflow of intellectual high spirits, a revel of debate, paradox, comedy and (above all) of invention, which starts many hares and kills none" (p. 169). Quoted in G. M. Logan, *The Meaning of More's "Utopia,"* Princeton, Princeton University Press, 1983, p. 5; see also on the same page (n. 4) Logan's references to others who see the work as a *jeu d'esprit*, to which may be added T. E. Bridgett, *The Life and Writings of Blessed Thomas More*, London, Burns, Oates & Washbourne, 1924, p. 105. See also J. W. Allen's characterization of Book II as a "fairy-tale" in *A History of Political Thought in the Sixteenth Century*, 1928; repr., London, Methuen, 1957, p. 154. G. H. Sabine in *A History of Political Theory* (New York, Holt, Rinehart and Winston, 1937), a text which has raised generations of first-year political science students, gives the down-side of the *jeu d'esprit* position. For him the *Utopia* is "pitiable," though a "worthy moral idea," because of its inability to "make its account with brute fact." He concludes: "For this reason the *Utopia* remained comparatively an isolated and unimportant episode in the political philosophy of its time. It illustrated rather the dying utterance of an old ideal than an authentic voice of the age that was coming into being" (p. 437).

3 The latest work in this tradition is Logan's *Meaning*. The Preface and Prolegomena discuss the major antecedents and contributors to this view.

4 The greatest proponent of this interpretation has been R. W. Chambers in his *Thomas More*, The Bedford Historical Series, London, Jonathan Cape, 1935. See also P. Albert Duhamel, "Medievalism in More's *Utopia*," *Studies in Philology*, 52 (1955). Duhamel sees the *Utopia* as "thoroughly Scholastic in its method of construction and largely medieval in its style and content . . . revealing the limitations of that method and of the society for which it was largely responsible" (p. 126). Discussions of the relation between Utopian institutions and monasticism are found in J. H. Hexter, *More's "Utopia": The Biography of an Idea*, 1952; repr. with an Epilogue, New York, Harper Torchbooks, 1965, pp. 85-91; F. E. Manuel and F. P. Manuel, *Utopian Thought in the Western World*, Cambridge, Mass., Harvard University Press, 1979, pp. 48-51; W. M. Gordon, "The Monastic Achievement and More's Utopian Dream," *Medievalia et Humanistica*, New Series, 9 (1979), pp. 199-214. See also the Yale ed., pp. xlv-l.

5 So Karl Kautsky, *Thomas More and His Utopia* (1st German ed., 1888), trans. H. J. Stenning, London, A. & C. Black, 1927; repr. with a Foreword by Russell Ames, New York, Russell & Russell, 1959. See also V. Volgin, "Sir Thomas More," *News, A Review of World Events*, 39, 15 February 1953, pp. 14-15; repr. in L. Gallagher, *More's Utopia and Its Critics*, Chicago, Scott, Foresman, 1964, pp. 106-08.

6 A number of interesting questions can be raised about the *Utopia* considered as a work
   of literature. These include the relation between More as actual author, implied
   author, and as a character in the work; between the objectivity which we might posit in
   an ideal reader and the actual readers of More's day and our own; an assessment of the
   effect of More's irony and satire and the related question of whether, or to what
   degree, he was intentionally ambiguous, contradictory, paradoxical or indulged in
   absurdity for its own sake. A good introduction to such concerns may be found in
   W. C. Booth's *The Rhetoric of Fiction*, Chicago, University of Chicago Press, 1961.
   All these questions can usefully be asked of the *Utopia*—although here only in an
   incidental sense, since I am looking at the work primarily for its contribution to the
   history of ideas. There are however important currents in contemporary literary
   criticism which will find my assumption—that there is an essential meaning and unity
   in the *Utopia*—naïve, and the effort to discover it misguided. Booth states this
   widely held position: "we have looked so long at foggy landscapes reflected in misty
   mirrors that we have come to *like* fog. Clarity and simplicity are suspect; irony reigns
   supreme" (p. 372). Life, according to this view, *is* ambiguous and contradictory so
   that a work of literature, such as the *Utopia*, is true in the degree that it reflects these
   ambiguities without attempting to reconcile them artificially—and besides this, there
   are as many versions of the meaning of such a work as there are readers, none of which
   is more "right" or more "wrong" than any other. Such a position accurately reflects
   our own inability to hold together the various parts of our world. But does this mean we
   should assume that More wrote from the same standpoint and for readers who thought
   as we do? The fundamental contract which makes all fiction possible is, as Jean-Louis
   Curtis said in criticizing Sartre's theory of the novel, "a tacit contract [of the reader]
   with the novelist, a contract granting him the right to know what he is writing about"
   (as reported by Booth, *Rhetoric of Fiction*, p. 52). This much we must grant
   More, so the only question is whether he *wrote*—i.e., intentionally or through
   incompetence—something that was profoundly inconsistent in which the various
   parts are not reconciled but merely juxtaposed. Aside from the unlikely anachronism
   of such a view, which supposes that More's world was just like our own, the only
   possible proof of my position lies in the pudding, i.e., it depends on whether or not we
   can find a single interpretation of the entire work which is both historically plausible
   and can account for all the elements in the text. This is what I am looking for.
7 These opinions are represented in the commendatory letters, etc. attached to the
   early editions. They are included in the Yale ed. We possess a number of other brief
   references to the *Utopia* such as the letter of Erasmus to Ulrich von Hutten of 23 July
   1517 in which he paints a word-picture of More. See *The Epistles of Erasmus, from His
   Earliest Letters to His Fifty-first Year*, 3 vols., trans. F. M. Nichols, New York,
   Russell and Russell, 1962, Vol. 3, pp. 387-402 (hereafter *Epistles*); on the date of this
   letter (1517 or 1519?), see Nichols' footnote, pp. 401-02. See also the various correspondence mentioned by Surtz in the Yale ed., pp. clxxxiii-cxc. The authoritative
   edition of Erasmus' letters is that of P. S. Allen, *Opus Epistolarum Des. Erasmi
   Roterodami*, 11 vols., Oxford, Clarendon Press, 1906-47, plus an index volume, 1958
   (hereafter *Opus Epistolarum*). This is the basis of Nichols' translations of selected
   letters as of the complete translation by R. A. B. Mynors et al. in *The Correspondence
   of Erasmus*, 1974-   (hereafter *Correspondence*), undertaken by the editors of the
   Collected Works of Erasmus, Toronto, University of Toronto Press. More had himself
   asked Erasmus to supply recommendations (for the first ed. of 1516) not only by
   scholars but especially by statesmen (Erasmus, *Opus Epistolarum*, Vol. 2, p. 346;
   trans. in *Correspondence*, Vol. 4, pp. 78-79). While it is true, as Hexter says, that
   these embody "interpretations of Utopia by a highly select group of More's contemporaries . . . all in close rapport with his intellectual ideals" (*More's "Utopia,"* p. 44), a
   broader testimony to the immediate popularity and comprehensibility of the work (see

below, n. 16) can be seen in the very large number of editions it went through in the century following its appearance: eleven—if one excludes the two of which there are no extant copies—as listed in J. G. T. Graesse, *Trésor des livres rares et précieux*, Milan, Ricordari, 1950, Vol. 4, p. 603. Details of the eleven editions are found in Surtz, Yale ed., pp. clxxxiii-cxcii.

8 As a first summation of this view of the meaning of *Utopia*, we can do no better than point to the words of Beatus Rhenanus where he says: "The *Utopia* contains principles of such a sort as it is not possible to find in your Plato, in Aristotle, or even in the *Pandects* of your Justinian. Its lessons are less philosophical, perhaps, than theirs but more Christian" (253/17-20). This letter also contains some of the only contemporary criticisms of the *Utopia*: that of the "dolt" (253/23) and those other "responsible" (253/22) "theologians" (253/33) who claimed More deserved no more credit for the book than was due to any scribe since all he did was to copy down what Hythloday said. Other criticism, which may only be More's own, is found in his second letter to Giles (see 249/1-253/7).

9 On the friends and acquaintances associated with the letters, etc. attached to the text, see P. R. Allen, "*Utopia* and European Humanism: The Function of the Prefatory Letters and Verses," *Studies in the Renaissance*, 10 (1963), 91-107. On the various stylistic clues which point to a humanist audience, see Logan's chapter, "The Letter to Giles," in *Meaning*, pp. 19-31.

10 Two of the best treatments of *Utopia* by this school may be found in J. H. Hexter's "Introduction," Part I in the Yale ed., pp. xv-cxxiv, and, more recently, Logan's *Meaning*. The latter contains extensive references to other works in this tradition.

11 Logan, *Meaning*, p. 3.

12 This formula, which became the actual title in the edition of March 1518, was contained in the nub of the titles in the two earlier editions. See the critical apparatus, Yale ed., p. 2.

13 For biographical details see Allen, "*Utopia* and European Humanism," and Surtz's discussion, the "Editions of *Utopia*," Part III in the Yale ed. (pp. clxxxiii-cxc).

14 Logan's highly sophisticated reading of the *Utopia*, which finds that its meaning could only be appreciated by the most erudite of Renaissance Humanists, forces him to reject (*Meaning*, pp. 25-26) the commonsense opinions (of Chambers, R. P. Adams and Skinner) that the *Utopia* was at least in part intended for an audience of Europeans in general (Chambers), all Englishmen (Adams), and the whole body of citizens (Skinner). On the divisions in More's audience, see also above, Preface, n. 2.

15 For a survey of the popularity of *Utopia*, see the Yale ed., p. cvi. Robinson's translation is included in J. H. Lupton's edition of *Utopia*.

16 Some readers may be inclined to question the implication that understanding is a necessary condition for popularity—having chiefly in mind the thought that, although the Bible is by far the most popular book ever written, this does not mean that it has been well understood since there are, notoriously, scores of conflicting interpretations. Or, as another reviewer asked, must we assume that "the many initial purchasers of Locke's *Essay Concerning Human Understanding* (for a while, a vogue book in England) understood it?" My answer to this second question is, in some sense, yes. For surely its popularity—or the popularity of any such work—means that, at the time, and regardless of whether or not every purchaser worked through the text, it was seen to be an important and therefore understandable work by those whom the age regarded as knowledgeable judges. Further, *our* experience that it is a "hard" book need not imply that it was so to Locke's contemporaries. Here the judgement of A. C. Fraser, in the Prolegomena to his magisterial edition of the *Essay* (Oxford, Clarendon Press, 1894; repr. New York, Dover Publications, 1959), is worth quoting: "The *Essay* rapidly attained a wide popularity, unprecedented in the case of an elaborate philosophical treatise, but explained by a relation of the book to life and action that could be

readily appreciated by persons unaccustomed to metaphysical speculation" (Vol. 1, p. xli).

On the other hand the case with the Bible is so unique that I think it has no real relation to what I say about the popularity of *Utopia*. The Bible is not popular (i.e., purchased) because it is held to be an amusing, useful and comprehensible work on a question of topical importance, but because it is seen as God's authoritative word which Christians are bound to try to understand. Furthermore, from at least the time of Augustine, there has been a strong tradition in Western theology which recognizes that this book, of all books, can be interpreted in a number of ways, all of which are true. With Augustine this does not mean that *any* interpretation is true but that, once false interpretations have been excluded, there can be a number of true interpretations of varying degrees of sophistication. In the *Confessions* (XII, xviiff.), for example, he lists five true meanings that can be given to the phrase of Genesis 1:1, "In the beginning God created the heaven and the earth." His teaching on this point deserves notice. He says: "how can it harm me that it should be possible to interpret these words in several ways, all of which may yet be true? How can it harm me if I understand the writer's meaning in a different sense from that in which another understands it? All of us who read his [Moses'] words do our best to discover and understand what he had in mind, and since we believe that he wrote the truth, we are not so rash as to suppose that he wrote anything which we know or think to be false. Provided, therefore, that each of us tries as best he can to understand in the Holy Scriptures what the writer meant by them, what harm is there if a reader believes what you, the Light of all truthful minds, shows him to be the true meaning? It may not even be the meaning which the writer had in mind, and yet he too saw in them a true meaning, different though it may be from this" (XII, xviii). Augustine expands on this position in the remainder of the book (XII), where it becomes clear that he is not stating the contemporary position that there is no one (or few) true meaning(s) because there are as many meanings as there are readers.

17   There are surprisingly few studies specifically devoted to the question of the relation of Plato and More given the fact that everyone recognizes the affinity. Among these the most detailed is still that of Lina Beger, "Thomas Morus und Platon: Ein Betrag zur Geschichte des Humanismus," *Zeitschrift für die gesammte Staatswissenschaft* (Tübingen), 35 (1879), 187-216, 405-83. More recently, see Thomas I. White, "Pride and the Public Good: Thomas More's Use of Plato in *Utopia*," *Journal of the History of Philosophy*, 20, 4 (October 1982). White (*ibid.*, p. 329, n. 1; p. 335, n. 13) gives a number of references to other works which examine the relationship, to which may be added Brendan Bradshaw, "More on Utopia," *The Historical Journal*, 24 (1981), esp. 14-26. See also J. D. Schaeffer, "Socratic Method in More's *Utopia*," *Moreana*, 69 (1981), 5-20. For a general treatment see Ernst Cassirer, *The Platonic Renaissance in England*, trans. J. P. Pettegrove, 1932; repr., New York, Thomas Nelson & Sons, 1953. Although concerned principally with the later Cambridge Platonists the work is useful for its discussion of the transmission of Platonism into England as well for what it has to say about More. A survey of the similarities between the *Republic* and *Utopia* is found in the introductions of both Hexter and Surtz in the Yale ed.; see esp. pp. xliv, lxxxvii-lxxxviii, cvii-cx, clvi-clx.

18   Giles identifies himself as the author of the *Tetrastichon* in his letter to Busleyden (23/22-25), but I do not understand why Logan speaks of Giles as the author of the *Hexastichon* (*Meaning*, p. 28), a conclusion which White ("Pride and the Public Good," p. 335, n. 13) also regards as "likely" without saying why.

19   The references are at 49/37; 87/19; 101/13; 103/16; 105/5 and 181/34. The marginal reference at 121/13 I take to be the work of Giles (see 23/25-26), but see the *caveat* to this obvious interpretation in the Yale ed., p. 280, 22/21.

20   Surtz (Yale ed., pp. clx-clxv) discusses briefly the influence of Plutarch, Lucian, Cicero, Seneca, Diogenes Laertius, Tacitus, Aristotle and others.

21 I argue this point in *Augustine's Conversion: A Commentary on the Argument of Books I-IX of the* Confessions, Waterloo, Ont., Wilfrid Laurier University Press, forthcoming, ch. 7.

22 Hexter's Introduction (Part I in the Yale ed.) displays the same tendency as Logan in his finding that More was far in advance of all his contemporaries (pp. xxvi-xxvii). Hexter finds that More taught a doctrine that did not really appear in Europe until some 200 years later with the *Philosophes* of the Enlightenment. Hexter writes, "More's contemporaries, especially the humanists, were inhibited from making a like combination [reason = virtue = nature] by the very form in which they usually cast their writing on politics. That form is the *Fürstenspiegel*, the Mirror of Princes.... Thus More breaks out of the circle which limited so much humanist writing about politics to platitudinous trivia and futile moralistic incantation" (pp. cxvi-cxvii).

23 More's intent in this regard is, I think, stated plainly in his second letter to Giles where he says, "I do not pretend that if I had determined to write about the commonwealth and had remembered such a story as I have recounted, I should have perhaps shrunk from a fiction whereby the truth, as if smeared with honey, might a little more pleasantly slide into men's minds" (251/5-9). That the work was in fact received as a witty and engaging piece is well attested in the various letters, etc. that accompany it.

24 See Hexter, *More's "Utopia."* He recapitulates, extends and modifies his argument in the Yale ed. (pp. xv-xxiii).

25 Erasmus, *Epistles*, Vol. 3, p. 398.

26 See Logan, *Meaning*, pp. 11-18. See also p. 27, n. 8, for his objection to A. R. Heiserman's attack ("Satire in the *Utopia*," *PMLA*, 78 [1983], 166) on Hexter's defence of the tradition that More wrote Book II in Flanders.

27 Hexter, *More's "Utopia,"* p. 28; quoted in Logan, *Meaning*, p. 15.

28 Hexter mentions Claude de Seyssel, *La Monarchie de France*, ed. Jacques Poujol, Paris, 1961, and Niccolò Machiavelli, *The Discourses* (Yale ed., p. xxxi). The list of authors and works concerned in one way or another with the question of how best to order a commonwealth can be greatly extended to include all those noted by Surtz (Yale ed., pp. clxxi-clxxix)—from Petrarch's *Africa* in the fourteenth century to Conrad Heresbach's *De educandis atque erudiendis principium liberis* (Torgau, 1598) in the sixteenth. The political writings of the time can be divided into those, like More's and Machiavelli's, which move to a modern solution and, on the other hand, the *speculum principis* genre which attempt, with an insistence that increases with their increasing futility, to bring the world back to the older forms.

29 By its judicious use of commentary and well-selected documents, Brian Tierney's *The Crisis of Church and State: 1050-1300* (Englewood Cliffs, N.J., Prentice-Hall, 1964) provides one of the best short accounts of the causes and consequences of the Investiture Controversy. A more detailed treatment may be found in R. W. and A. J. Carlyle's *A History of Medieval Political Thought in the West*, Vols. 4 and 5, Edinburgh and London, William Blackwood & Sons, 1930.

30 Johan Huizinga's *Waning of the Middle Ages* is the classic study of the general consequences of the increasing confusion and imbalance between the sacred and secular in the period 1300-1500 (trans. F. Hopman, 1924; repr., Garden City, N.Y., Doubleday Anchor Books, 1954).

31 See Machiavelli, *The Prince, A Bilingual Edition*, trans. and ed. Mark Musa, New York, St. Martin's Press, 1964, ch. xxv, for his summary of the confusion of his times which had induced men to give up any hope of bringing about a reform.

32 Ambrose and Augustine defined the relationship between church and state that became normative in the West throughout the Middle Ages. The Western Empire was to be ruled by a partnership of *two* separate powers—the church and the state. Ambrose insisted on this successfully when he excommunicated the emperor Theodosius (390) and did not readmit him to communion until he had done public penance in the cathedral at Milan. See the brief account of the episode in Ferdinand

Lot, *The End of the Ancient World and the Beginnings of the Middle Ages*, trans. P. and M. Leon, 1931; repr., New York, Harper Torchbooks, 1961, p. 196. Ambrose writes of the matter in his *Letter LI* (to Theodosius), available in English in *Nicene and Post-Nicene Fathers*, 2nd series, Vol. 10, Grand Rapids, Mich., Wm. B. Eerd-mans, 1955, p. 450. Augustine worked out the separation and relation of the two powers in his vastly influential *City of God* (written 413-26); see esp. XIX, 14-17. The classic formulation of the two-power theory—with the pope and emperor as the respective heads—comes in the letter of Pope Gelasius I to the Emperor Anastasius (494). The relevant text is reproduced in Tierney, *Church and State*, pp. 13-14.

33 R. P. Adams (*The Better Part of Valor: More, Erasmus, Colet, and Vives on Humanism, War, and Peace, 1496-1535*, Seattle, University of Washington Press, 1962) remarks (p. 122) that "The *Utopia* . . . appeared when England was at peace and when a rather well-tempered humanistic optimism existed, based on the hope that, at least in England, peace might continue and that a golden age of social reform might yet be possible." See also ch. 10 (pp. 158-85): "Henry VIII 'seems extremely desirous of peace' (1517-1520)," in which Adams describes the hopes of the humanists up to the Field of the Cloth of Gold in 1520.

In 1509 More had, on the occasion of Henry VIII's coronation (24 June 1509), written of his accession to the throne that this was the beginning of the return of the golden age foretold by Plato—see no. 22 in *Latin Poems*, in *The Complete Works of St. Thomas More*, ed. C. H. Miller, L. Bradner, C. A. Lynch, R. P. Oliver, Vol. 3, Part II, New Haven, Yale University Press, 1984 (hereafter *Latin Poems*). Even making due allowances for the formal and hyperbolical nature of More's praise of Henry, which at the time was probably more sincere than otherwise, what remains is that as early as 1509 More, in some sort, saw the possibility of a return of Plato's golden age which, as I will argue, More equated with the Arcadian paradise of the *Republic*. By 1516 he may no longer have cherished much hope that Henry was about to usher it in, if we may judge by the last lines of the *Utopia* (247/1-3), but his book was a blueprint of what it would look like. Erasmus, in a letter of 1517 to Guolfangus Fabritius Capito (originally, Wolfgang Schmied, who changed his name at Erasmus' suggestion, first to Wolfangus Faber and then to the form above), could still say, "I could almost wish to be young again, for no other reason but this, that I anticipate the near approach of a golden age; so clearly do we see the minds of princes, as if changed by inspiration, devoting all their energies to the pursuit of peace" (*Epistles*, Vol. 2, p. 506). On this day his hopes rested on the Pope and the King of France but Erasmus was very mercurial on the subject, as the next letter shows.

See the Appendix for my objections to Hexter's account of More's visit to Antwerp in 1515.

34 These include the *Tetrastichon* in the Utopian alphabet with its Latin translation (which Giles "added to the book," 23/21-26), Giles' letter to Busleyden, and Giles' marginal notes which include one of the seven occasions where Plato's name is mentioned in the text. See above, n. 19, for these references.

More's undated poem no. 198 (*Latin Poems*), published in the March and December 1518 editions of the *Utopia*, discusses the question of the best form of rule under the clearly Platonic title *OPTIMUS REIPUB. STATUS*.

35 Yale ed., p. cxvii, quoted above, n. 22; cf. with Hexter's characterization of the form as "wretched and dreary" in *More's "Utopia,"* p. 103. The breakdown of the older principle is what made the Mirror of Princes of the era so incompetent. Surtz discusses some Renaissance exemplars, Yale ed., pp. clxxi-clxxix. See also Logan's well-founded objections to seeing *Utopia* as a *speculum principis* (*Meaning*, pp. 23-26, and the other locations cited in the Index). Erasmus' *The Education of a Christian Prince*, contemporary with both *Utopia* and *The Prince*, is available in English in the translation of L. K. Born, Records of Civilization, Sources and Studies, 1936; repr., New

York, W. W. Norton, 1968. See R. P. Adams (*The Better Part of Valor*, ch. 7) for a sympathetic account of Erasmus' aim in the *Christian Prince* and pp. 164-68 for a similar account of the *Complaint of Peace, Unwanted and Ejected from All Countries* (1517), in which Erasmus tries to persuade both princes and people of the folly of "glory" in chivalric war and the depravity of a "brave" soldiery. Adams' intention is otherwise but, by setting these works in the historical context of the *realpolitik* of the day, he only underscores their fatuity.

36 On the importance of these works in Renaissance political thought see Yale ed., p. clxiii.

37 On Renaissance Platonism in general, see Paul Oskar Kristeller's *Renaissance Thought: The Classic, Scholastic and Humanist Strains*, New York, Harper Torchbooks, 1961, pp. 48-69. On Ficino, see the same author's *The Philosophy of Marsilio Ficino*, trans. V. Conant, New York, Columbia University Press, 1943. On Colet, see J. H. Lupton, *A Life of John Colet . . . with an Appendix of Some of His English Writings*, London, 1887; 2nd ed. repr., Hamden, Conn., Shoe String Press, 1961.

38 Erasmus to Ulrich von Hutten, *Epistles*, Vol. 3, p. 398.

39 Thomas Stapleton, *The Life and Illustrious Martyrdom of Sir Thomas More*, trans. Philip E. Hallett, London, 1928, p. 15 (Stapleton-Hallett, ed. E. E. Reynolds, has been reprinted, London, Burns & Oates, 1966). See also the references to More and Plato, Yale ed., p. clvii, n. 1.

40 Augustine, *City of God*, VIII, 7-12. See also II, 14 where he says of the *Republic*, "Plato . . . when he was sketching his rational idea of a perfect commonwealth . . . ." This gives us a clear idea of Augustine's perception of, and high regard for, Plato's political philosophy (trans. H. Bettenson, Harmondsworth, Penguin, 1972, p. 63).

41 Augustine, *City of God*, VIII, 9.

42 Erasmus to Ulrich von Hutten (*Epistles*, Vol. 3, p. 393). These lectures were given—c. 1501—in Grocyn's Church of St. Lawrence in the Old Jewry (William Roper, *The Lyfe of Sir Thomas More*, ed. E. V. Hitchcock, Oxford: Early English Text Society, 1935, p. 6). Stapleton (*Life*, pp. 7-8) says that More treated the *City of God* "not . . . from the theological point of view, but from the standpoint of history and philosophy." On the great importance of Augustine to the Renaissance Humanists, see Kristeller, *Renaissance Thought*, pp. 82-86.

43 I do not mean that More's preference for Plato is to be taken exclusively but rather in the exact sense of Augustine (*City of God*, VIII, 9), that Plato was taken as the spokesman for all those philosophers who have come to the truth.

44 See Hexter, Yale ed., pp. xxxiii-xli.

45 So Logan, *Meaning*, p. 16. Hexter's earlier position is found in his *More's "Utopia."*

46 Hexter, Yale ed., p. xxvi.

47 See *ibid.*, pp. cxi-cxiii.

48 Evidence that it was an afterthought is contained in Erasmus' letter to von Hutten where he says, "He had written the second book at his leisure, and *afterwards*, when he found it was *required*, added the first off-hand" (emphasis mine; *Epistles*, Vol. 3, p. 398). In other words the discovery that more was required came only after More had finished the second book.

COMMENTARY ON BOOK I
OF MORE'S *UTOPIA*

A number of commentators have noted similarities between the beginning of *Utopia* and the setting of the *Republic*. Besides the dialogue form, "which is an obvious Platonic contribution to the *Utopia*," Surtz notes that "The interlocutors in both the *Republic* and the *Utopia* repair to a private residence after a religious ceremony in a seaport."[1] The similarity goes very much deeper.

In the *Republic* the religious festival being held in the Piraeus was concerned with the introduction of the cult of a foreign goddess, Bendis, from semi-barbarous Thrace.[2] Plato does this to suggest the setting in which the problem of the first book had arisen. Its question "What is justice?" had become pressing through Athens' assimilation—partly because of its sea-faring orientation—of a whole variety of foreign gods and alien ideas. These, by their comparison with the established order, had raised questions and shaken the old assumptions—issuing in the Sophistic movement. This was as attractive to the young as it was dangerous to the city—both of which Plato illustrates in the discussion which follows.

In this, the old order is represented by Cephalus whose opinions are entirely traditional. He assumes the existence of an objective and divine order revealed to the poets to whose authority he defers in every word. He first quotes, with approval, the saying of Sophocles that old age is a blessing because it frees us from the passions of youth as "from a raging and savage beast of a master" (329c). This shows his philosophical spirit in that—unlike the other old men of his circle who merely bemoan the loss of vigour as if it were the whole good (329a)—he sets the passing of his natural forces, along with the rest of his life, in relation to an absolute

---

Reference notes to the Commentary appear on pp. 74-89.

divine order represented by Hades.[3] For Cephalus old age is therefore a kind of inducement to philosophy, leading us to wonder if we are in a right relation to the demands of the gods below who may soon judge us by *their* standard. He approves Pindar's words concerning the consolations of hope in a just and pious life (331a,b) but proves unable to state what justice is in every case. His definition, which Socrates actually formulates—"to tell the truth and return what one has received" (331d)—is, in the end of Plato's argument, shown to be true when taken in the sense of a harmony between the parts of a whole in which each gets its due (see 443d,e as the conclusion of the argument in Books I-IV) and then, further, when it has been shorn of every externality through the discovery of the intelligible Forms (Book V and following). But here, held in the manner Cephalus holds it—as a true opinion—it has become personal and divisive. He is not troubled by the inadequacy of his definition, even though he agrees with Socrates that it would not be right to return a weapon to a man who has gone mad (331c,d), but is content to hand over the argument to his son Polemarchus so that he can go off and *do* the just thing by attending the sacrifices (331d). However true his opinion may be it is clear that he holds it as if it had reference to himself alone (i.e., in the justice *he* can afford through the pious use of his wealth), and as if it entailed no responsibility to anyone else— neither to the members of his family nor to the wider community—since he neither urges them to the sacrifices nor tries to resolve the difficulty suggested by Socrates. Thus Plato shows a division in the city between the old men like Cephalus who suppose they know what justice is, and try to do it, but who see no need to argue about it even while they allow the inadequacy of their view in certain cases[4] and, on the other hand, the younger men who see no reason to attend the sacrifices like their fathers—whose views are not taken as authoritative because there are many exceptions and many competing definitions—but who are attracted by an argument about justice in which they hope to shine. To this point everything is still friendly and good-natured but the dangerous consequences implicit in this division are brought out with increasing clarity by the next two speakers.

Polemarchus, exactly half-way between the traditional assumptions of his father and the new Sophistic position of the third speaker, Thrasymachus, begins, like Cephalus, by referring to the poets as authorities for the definition he proposes (Simonides, at 331d). Under Socrates' questioning he soon reveals that he does not think the authority of the poets is grounded in their divine inspiration. Rather, it is determined simply by the worldly utility of what they recommend. Socrates easily shows that on such a premise no definition of justice is possible since it lacks any stability and becomes different things in relation to the differing circumstances and understanding of every individual. Polemarchus ends up in confusion, denying what he first affirmed, and concluding that no truly wise authority could have meant what he had supposed the poets to mean.[5] The remainder of the book is concerned with Thrasymachus as the radical representative of the new Sophistic position. Where Cephalus accepted a divine authority, literally without question, and Polemarchus thought to give rational arguments for a definition received on divine authority—only to end up not knowing what he meant—Thrasymachus systematically rejects every assumption that there is any binding objective order from the gods with the result that justice "is nothing else than the advantage of the stronger" (338c). A position such as this, if widely accepted, threatened the complete destruction of Athens. The ferocious images Plato uses to describe Thrasymachus underscore the danger: "gathering himself up like a wild beast he hurled himself upon us as if he would tear us to pieces" (336b). And so he and his kind would have—unless Plato could find and maintain another definition of justice.

In the long discussion to the end of Book I Socrates manages to bring various objections to Thrasymachus' definition which, as he is more and more unable to answer them, silence Thrasymachus but without convincing him and thus without removing the threat. The book ends with Socrates' own admission that, although they have found difficulties with all the current definitions of justice (as proposed by Cephalus, Polemarchus and Thrasymachus), he is still as far as ever from knowing what justice itself really is (see 354b). This is true, yet by raising the contradictions in the current notions Socrates has implicitly established that the only satisfactory idea of justice will be the one which is thinkable—i.e., a self-related notion with the form of pure thought that does not depend on a relation to anything other than itself (such as Cephalus' simple idea of returning what one has received, or Thrasymachus' confused ideas about the interest of the stronger), by which any definition may easily be brought into self-contradiction.

The second book begins with the challenge of Glaucon and Adimantus that, instead of considering the opinions various men have about justice, some of which now appear to have little or no relation to what it actually is, Socrates should lead them to a scientific inquiry aimed at discovering what justice is in itself. He should do this with no consideration of the opinions men have of it (see 357a-367e). Socrates takes up the challenge by suggesting that, since justice has so far proven difficult to discern when looked for in relation to individual men (i.e., is it just for Cephalus to return a weapon to someone who has gone mad), they should look first to where it admittedly exists in a larger form, i.e., in a state, "and then only examine it also in the individual looking for the likeness of the greater in the form of the less" (369a). From this he goes on to propose that if they could observe the origins of a state they might also be able to discern the origin and nature of justice and injustice in it. With this he turns to the famous consideration of the elements of a state which becomes the basis of the argument in the remainder of the *Republic*.

More's purpose in the first book of the *Utopia* is the same as Plato's in the first book of the *Republic*. It suggests the setting in which a problem had arisen and argues against the adequacy of any existing solution. In this way in both texts the first book clears the ground for the radically new structure the authors propose as the true answer to their respective problems: in Plato's case, in his examination of the origin of a state as the place to discover what justice is; in More's, to the island of Utopia as the place to discover what the best commonwealth might be. The trick is that what More took to be Plato's *solution*—i.e., the separation of the three classes and the rule of a philosopher king—now appeared in the sixteenth century as the *problem*.[6] The first book of the *Utopia* is thus a refutation of Plato's solution in its original form as this was read by More and his contemporaries. In the second, in the island of Utopia, More offers the true version of Plato's answer—purified and corrected by the light of a millennium and a half of Christianity.

For More the details of the setting are as telling as they are for Plato. No one in England or the Low Countries could have been ignorant of the calamitous problems raised on a world-wide scale by the new mercantilism. Growing up largely outside the forms of the Middle Ages, these purely economic interests had already torn the internal fabric of both countries and threatened ultimately to involve them in war. Henry VIII—referred to in the opening sentence of *Utopia* by the martial title of *invictissimus Anglicae rex*, "the most invincible king of England" (46/8-9)[7]—had sent an embassy to Bruges to try and straighten out these "weighty matters" (47/10)—i.e., the increasingly strained commercial relations between England and the Low Countries (Flanders, Zeeland, Brabant) following the failure of an earlier embassy in 1512. The purpose of the mission, which included More, was to renegotiate the old commercial treaties dating from 1496 and 1506—known as the treaties of intercourse (*Intercursus Magnus*, 1496; *Intercursus Malus*, 1506)— concerning, especially, the export of English wool and cloth to the Netherlands.[8] And not a moment too soon! The English ambassadors to the court of Charles, Prince of Castile (later, the Holy Roman Emperor, Charles V), had been informed by his chancellor, Jean le Sauvage, in June of the preceding year (1514), that the last day for renegotiating the treaty would be 1 October 1514—after which all English goods discovered in Flanders would be confiscated. The ambassadors, William Knight and Edward Poynings, had arranged for a brief prolongation of the *status quo* until 24 June 1515 but the threat to English interests remained very great. It seems indeed that the Netherlanders agreed to this prolongation only in the hopes that they could use the time to negotiate a general treaty of friendship or amity between Henry and Charles as well as another between Charles and the French.[9] Taken together, they expected these alliances to protect them when they then carried out their real intention of attacking on the commercial front by seizing all English goods on 24 June in 1515.[10] In February of 1515 Wolsey was informed by letter from the Duke of Suffolk (Charles Brandon), Nicholas West, and Richard Wingfield that:

> it is to be feared that the Prince of Castile and his Council that now ruleth about him, upon pride of the said alliance and amity [with France], woll suddenly arrest the English fleet and cast on the merchant's necks all the arrearages of the Sewestoll and the toll of the Hound, which ammounteth to a marvellous great sum, not able to be paid by our merchants without their utter undoing.[11]

By setting the *Utopia* in the context of these negotiations over the wool trade, More, as explicitly as Plato,[12] intended to evoke in the minds of his contemporaries the source of the danger that threatened the violent destruction of nations. For Plato the danger came through the assimilation of foreign gods and principles and from the questions they raised. More is equally precise in locating the source of the danger in the new mercantile spirit embodied, in Northern Europe in the sixteenth century, above all in the wool industry. On both sides everyone knew that if the merchants of England or the Netherlands were ruined this would involve the ruin of the whole system beneath them in their respective countries. In England this would lead to the collapse of the industry which had become the backbone of its economy[13] and, in the Netherlands, to the ruin of the wool-finishing and cloth trades which were the mainstay of her highly developed town life.[14] The degree to which these consequences were realized on either side was the degree to which war would become inevitable.

Against this, and again like Plato, More is careful to show in the setting those things which also united the parties divided in the dispute. In the *Republic* these elements are provided partly from the old order—in the gracious hospitality of Cephalus, himself, appropriately, a foreigner whose house, like a microcosm of Athens, provided a place where differing views could mingle—and partly also by the new order as seen in the interest of those present to resolve the question through philosophical argument. More shows the same two things. What the divided parties shared from the old order was the Christian religion which More specifically mentions (49/17-18), indicating thereby that he found it in the Low Countries the same as in England. What they shared that was new was the common attachment, of at least some on each side, to the ideals of Renaissance Humanism. This he makes clear by his praise and admiration for the leading characters of *each* mission: Cuthbert Tunstal on the English side, and Georges de Themsecke who, though not the actual head of the Netherlands mission, was their "chief speaker and guiding spirit" (47/26).[15] On a less exalted plane he stresses the same bond between himself, as an Englishman educated in the new spirit, and the similarly enlightened "Peter Giles, a native of Antwerp" (49/2-3). From the beginning the principles of Christianity and the new humanism—which, to be sure, were the ultimate source of the danger—are also the points to which he will look for its solution.

This then is the setting of the Dialogue of Book I in which Raphael Hythlodaeus plays the part—corresponding to Socrates' role in the first book of the *Republic*—of criticizing contemporary attempts to understand and answer the problem. In the course of the Dialogue the problem itself becomes ever more clear and explicit, as is the case in the *Republic*. More begins with a brief sketch of the character of Raphael who is able to fulfil Socrates' role because, above all else, his is a "good [*generosus*] and truly philosophic spirit" (57/11). Many commentators have noted that "More characterizes Hythloday largely in terms of traditional attributes of the philosopher"[16] without also noting that More intended his learned readers to see Raphael's position as similar to that of Socrates in the Platonic *Republic*.

As in Plato's well-known judgement of Socrates, Raphael is described by More—already in the title of Book I—as a *vir eximius*, "an extraordinary man" (47/2). He is such because, like Socrates, he had "devoted himself entirely to philosophy" (51/2), was "desirous neither of riches nor of power" (57/8) and, having freed himself from his family concerns (55/11-12) and refusing to enter political life (57/1, to the end of Book I), had given himself over to the discovery and dissemination of the truth in human affairs regardless of any danger of death (51/11-12) or of any personal preference. We know this last point because Raphael tells us later that he "would never have wished to leave [Utopia] except to make known that new world" (107/21-22); i.e., he left Utopia, where he wanted to stay, solely to teach Europe. Further, like Socrates, Raphael was indifferent to outward appearances (49/20-23) and, like Socrates in his speech who "only cares if his matter is correct and leaves his manner to take care of itself" (*Symposium* 199b), Raphael too, though "endowed with no ordinary powers of expression" (21/25-26), nevertheless had a careless simplicity of style (39/13-14) and would never knowingly depart from the truth for reasons of expediency (101/5-11).[17] Finally, Raphael's name itself is, I think, intended as a reference to Socrates.[18] His Christian name links him with the archangel Raphael and means "the healing of God" while Hythlodaeus was made up by More from two Greek roots—most probably ὕθλος, "nonsense" and δάιος, "knowing." If all this is run together, his name would mean something like "the healing (one) of God, knowing nonsense." This is an almost literal restatement of Socrates' own description of the beginning and end of his career, as one sent by God to heal the Athenians (see *Apology* 31b, "sent to this city as a gift of God"), who in the end both knew and said that he knew nothing but the nonsense of those who claimed they were wise (see *Apology* 23b, where he imagines the oracle as saying, "The wisest of you men is he who has realized, like Socrates, that in respect of wisdom he is really worthless").

In spite of this More had to make one significant alteration from the Platonic Socrates in order to adapt Raphael to play the Socratic role in the context of the intellectual climate of sixteenth-century Europe. For Plato, Socrates was the wisest man in Greece (*Apology* 21a) and was the embodiment of the philosopher not *because* of his wide experience — Socrates had never left Athens (*Crito* 52b) — but because, pre-eminently in his time, he moved *away* from experience and appearances and inwards towards the discovery of intelligible truth. For More the precise opposite was the case. If Raphael was to be recognized by the men of the Renaissance as the most perfect philosopher and the wisest man in Europe, then this would depend on his being not the least, but the most experienced of men. The reason is that for More and all his contemporaries the discovery of an absolute truth was not the problem. They knew themselves as holding this already from the Christian religion. Jesus Christ, who was God Incarnate, had taught and shown everything man needed to know. For them, the real problem lay in the precise and detailed application of that truth to every moment and circumstance of worldly life. For this task the wisest man would be the one who had experienced the most—who knew best what actually happens *in fact* when one tries to embody the truth in this way or in that. As Cardinal Morton says to Raphael (87/7-18), it is not possible in such questions to know in advance by any abstract reasoning what will work. Where the end sought is in particular events in time and space, reason, which apprehends only universals, has no place and experience and experiment are all.

More therefore presents Raphael as the most experienced man in Europe: "There is no mortal alive today who can give you such an account of unknown peoples and lands" (49/30-32). In the very act of introducing Raphael to More, Giles, giving as it were his qualifications, stresses his extraordinary travels and their philosophical nature (49/27-50/21). He makes this point when he corrects More who, from Raphael's appearance and dress, had guessed he was a ship's captain (49/34-35). " 'But you are quite mistaken,' said he, 'for his sailing has not been like that of Palinurus but that of Ulysses or, rather, of Plato' " (49/36-37). His point is that while Palinurus, helmsman of Aeneas on the great voyage from Troy to Italy, had travelled much he had done so only in his capacity as a ship's captain. His interest was exclusively in the business of sailing and piloting Aeneas' fleet.[19] The travels of Raphael, who comes from Portugal (51/4)—and thus from that nation which began the modern European exploration of the world[20]—were not at all like this. In Giles' precise specification they were like those of Ulysses or, rather, of Plato. The mention of both these names is not rhetorical. Neither alone conveys a precise analogy to Raphael's voyages: together they do.

To the late Middle Ages Ulysses was the epitome of the world's most travelled man.[21] He is used here as such—and Giles, in his letter to Busleyden, says that, "To my mind he [Raphael] was a man superior even to Ulysses in his knowledge of countries, men and affairs" (21/ 29-31)—i.e., superior in this respect to any man of former times. The same was also true of any modern, since Giles goes on to say, "in comparison with him Vespucci himself [the most widely travelled man of the day] may be thought to have seen nothing" (21/32-33).[22] Unlike Palinurus, Ulysses had a strong intellectual curiosity in all the peoples and places he came to—of which the most striking evidence is the episode where he had himself lashed to the mast to hear the singing of the Sirens while his men, their ears stopped with wax, rowed immune to their fatal song (*Odyssey* XII,39ff.). Partly this curiosity was reflected in Raphael and partly not, and the difference was twofold. Like Ulysses in this incident,[23] Raphael set out freely (51/8-12) in search of knowledge and experience but unlike Ulysses with the Sirens, he never did so from a merely idle curiosity. The tales of Ulysses' voyage include much of a fabulous nature and Raphael reported nothing of the kind. This was much to More's liking, who dismisses such things as unedifying: "about stale traveller's wonders we were not curious. Scyllas and greedy Celaenos and folk-devouring Laestrygones and similar frightful monsters are common enough, but well and wisely trained citizens are not everywhere to be found" (53/36-39).[24]

The last clause indicates the sense in which Plato's travels provide a better analogy to Raphael's voyages than do those of Ulysses, even though, in respect to the variety of places visited, Ulysses was more like Raphael than was Plato. The point is that More understood Plato to have undertaken his travels freely with the sole and exclusive intent of learning or teaching, like Raphael, "those wise and prudent provisions which he noticed anywhere among nations living together in a civilized way" (53/33-34).[25] Raphael then is like Plato in the philosophical quality of his travels and like Ulysses in respect to their quantity—and both of these are distinguished from the travels of a ship's captain such as Palinurus.

After this brief but complete introduction More turns swiftly to the argument of the first book, relating the conversation which led Raphael to mention Utopia (55/5-8). This discussion began when Peter Giles "wondered" that Raphael did not attach himself to the service of some king (55/15-22). Like Plato, More, with playful subtlety but great precision, locates the origin of his philosophy in wonder (see *Theatetus*, 155d: "This sense of wonder is the mark of the philosopher. Philosophy indeed has no other origin...").[26]

Hexter's discovery of the compositional seam which occurs at just this point,[27] and which has been widely accepted, has tended to fracture the work even for a scholar such as Logan who wants to see it as a unity. Logan finds Hexter's claim, that at this point More opened a seam in an earlier form of the work in order to insert new material, "incontestable" and goes on to note that "More's patchwork here is quite crude" (*Meaning*, p. 52). This is not so if, instead of focusing on the seam and the inserted material, one attends only to what More has actually put before the reader.

If we look at this we see that the *Utopia*, taken as a whole, reports the conversations More and Giles had with Raphael between the end of morning service in Notre Dame (49/17) until just before supper 245/33). This talk was divided into three blocks. First, there was a long discussion in the morning, immediately after their meeting, in which More and Giles "eagerly inquired of him [Raphael], and he no less readily discoursed" (53/35-36) on, above all, "those wise and prudent provisions which he noticed anywhere among nations living together in a civilized way" (53/33-34). More reports little of this conversation apart from the travel arrangements and geographical facts (see 51/29-53/29) but we can infer its content on two further points. At no time in *this* conversation was Utopia mentioned, and it was sufficiently interesting to prompt Peter Giles, on the basis of what he was hearing, to wonder why Raphael had not gone into the service of a Prince. This comment led directly to the second main division of the day's talk, occupying the rest of the morning until lunch (109/29). This part is reported in its entirety in the remainder of Book I (from 55/15-109/31). There are two points to note about this part of the day's conversation. Its major concern is with the question of whether or not a philosopher such as Raphael should place his knowledge in the service of a king. And the dialogue that ensued, beginning with Giles' speech at 55/15, was in More's express statement distinguished from their earlier talk by the fact that it was *this* discussion, and this alone, that "led Raphael on to mention that commonwealth [i.e., Utopia]" (55/7-8). This means that the Dialogue of Book I—however much it may have been written later and inserted in an earlier version of the work—was specifically and explicitly intended by More as *preparatory* to the description of Utopia.

I have no quarrel with Hexter's account of the seam nor with his locating it where he does.[28] But it seems that only a misreading of the text can lead to his conclusion that the inserted work is discontinuous with Book II, or to Logan's that "More's patchwork here is quite crude" (*Meaning*, p. 12). Hexter located the seam at this point because at 54/5-6 More says, "Now I intend to relate merely what he [Raphael] told us about the manners and customs of the Utopians." This would lead the reader to expect that the account of Utopia (in Book II) would follow immediately. But this is *not* what happens and, for the remainder of Book I, More appears to speak at length—in his treatment of the Achorians, Macarians and Polylerites—of what he had just said he would not discuss (53/30-31)—i.e., "the wise and prudent provisions which he [Raphael] noticed anywhere among nations living together in a civilized way" (53/33-34). Because of this apparent discrepancy, Hexter and Logan conclude that, in a rather careless manner, More opened up the text at this point and added the new material which he had written in London to the earlier-written Introduction and the Discourse on Utopia. On the face of it this is plausible enough but it is *only* the case (a) if one ignores the weight of More's statement that, *before* going on to tell of the manners and customs of the Utopians, he intended "first . . . [to give] the talk which drew and led him [Raphael] on to mention that common-wealth" (55/6-8), and (b) if one is obliged to suppose that the mention of the wise and prudent provisions among the Achorians, Macarians and Polylerites that does follow were in fact amongst those things Raphael had spoken of *earlier*—in the first (unreported) part of the morning conversation. Only on these conditions is there any discrepancy between what More says he will do and what he does.

But there is no reason to ignore More's statement of how he will proceed nor to make this supposition. If the reader does neither, the argument flows without a hitch. That is, the first part of the day's conversation, which More does not report, included the mention of some of the wise and prudent provisions which Raphael noted in his travels. These instances More says he "must mention on another occa-sion" (55/4-5), i.e., beyond this work. There is nothing to support the supposition that in this part of the discussion Raphael made any mention of the Achorians, Macarians or Polylerites. As the sequel shows they certainly had many wise provisions—but nothing obliges us to suppose that Raphael had spoken a word about these nations in the first part of the day's conversation. If the good and bad features Raphael discussed in this first, unreported, section were of any peoples *other than* the Achorians, Macarians and Polylerites then, when More says that he now intends, passing this material over, to concentrate instead on the con-versation which led up to the mention of Utopia (55/5-8), he is freed of any crudeness or inconsistency. On this reading, the wise provisions of these three peoples which do form part of the reported discussion, and do lead to the mention of Utopia, will be seen as something Raphael had not talked about before and so the mention of them would not be a *return* to material More said he would not discuss—as supposed by Hexter and Logan. Since there is no necessity for making this supposition we shall abandon it.

The seam therefore remains but not the claim that More's patchwork is crude (i.e., containing an obvious discrepancy) nor, worse, Hexter's contention that the work is not a unity (being destroyed by the insertion of foreign material). Rather, we must look to see how—far from being alien to the description of Utopia—*all* the inserted material leads logically to Raphael's mention of the island commonwealth at the end of the morning's discussion. It seems clear that More thought it served this function and this is the sole reason why he included a full report on just *this* part of the morning's conversation in his book on Utopia. Hexter seems thus to have located his seam at the right point but for the wrong reasons.

The third division of the day's discussion occurred only after the conversation in the second had led Raphael to mention Utopia on several occasions in such a way that the argument could not proceed without a full account of that commonwealth. Raphael gave this at length, after lunch and before supper, and it is related by More in the second book.

The question we must now ask is why More felt he must add the argument of the Dialogue in Book I in order to prepare the reader for the account of Utopia in Book II. The answer is not difficult. We have only to imagine how the book would appear to his readers if it had consisted simply of the Introduction and Raphael's description of Utopia. The reader's difficulties in understanding what More was saying would then be exactly the same as the difficulties Raphael says he would face in having his advice taken seriously in the councils of kings. "To sum it all up," he says of his argument in Book I, "if I tried to obtrude these and the like ideas on men strongly inclined to the opposite way of thinking, to what deaf ears should I tell the tale!" (97/35-38). This is a point with which More heartily agreed:

> "Deaf indeed, without doubt," I agreed, "and, by heaven, I am not surprised. Neither, to tell the truth, do I think that such ideas should be thrust upon people, or such advice given, as you are positive will never be listened to. What good could such novel ideas do, or how could they enter the minds of individuals who are already taken up and possessed of the opposite conviction?" (97/39-99/5)

I think we can be fairly certain here that More, the character in the *Utopia*, is expressing the opinion of More the author just because the latter did take the trouble to add the argument of Book I to the already-written Introduction and Discourse on Utopia. Such incomprehension on the part of his readers would certainly have been the result if More had merely presented Raphael's description of Utopia. Coming literally from another world, its ideas would have had no chance of being seriously considered unless their relation to the actual situation of his readers was first established.[29] This is the function of the Dialogue of Book I. It is intended to prepare the reader to receive a new and truer position by first showing the inadequate nature of the traditional solutions based on what had become received truths and long-unexamined presuppositions.

I. More's Criticism of the Platonic Separation of the Classes

Let us now turn to the argument of the Dialogue in Book I beginning at 55/15. In it Raphael, speaking for More the author, aims to show that the two most essential features of the old order are in fact the cause of the problems in contemporary Europe. Both were ultimately derived from the teaching of Plato's *Republic*. Raphael attacks the Platonic dogma that ''commonwealths will finally be happy only if either philosophers become kings or kings turn to philosophy'' (87/12-13; see *Republic* 473c,d; 499b,c), *and* he criticizes the notion that there can be no true republic where the Platonic distinction between the three classes of philosopher-king, guardians and craftsmen was not observed (see *Republic* II-IV).

Raphael first attacks the necessity of separating the three classes in the episode at Cardinal Morton's (59/19-85/38) where the traditional (i.e., Platonic) position is defended by the pompous lawyer. His argument against the desirability of a philosopher-king begins after this when he turns the conversation to the problem of counselling a king (87/26). Here the character More argues against Raphael in favour of the traditional (i.e., Platonic) position that there can only be ''a distant prospect of happiness if philosophers will not condescend even to impart their counsel to kings'' (87/13-15).

The Dialogue begins with Giles' astonishment that Raphael, the quintessential philosopher, did not ''attach himself to some king'' (55/15-16) where his learning and experience would surely be welcome as entertaining and also, possibly, of some assistance. This, says Giles, ''would not only serve [Raphael's] own interests excellently but [would] be of great assistance in the advancement of all [his] relatives and friends'' (55/20-22). In this remark we start with the very lowest view of the philosopher and the highest view of the king which is, no doubt, the position More thought most of his readers actually held. The philosopher here is merely an entertainer who might accidentally be of assistance to the king by "furnishing him with examples" (55/19) and he is thought to be moved by the most vulgar, immediate and sophistic of reasons—personal gain and the advancement of his family. The king, on the other hand, who has all power and knowledge and needs the philosopher only to divert and "amuse" himself (*oblectare*, 54/16), is exalted to the highest position. It is no wonder that Raphael, spurning this suggestion, calls it not serviced but "servitude" (*servitium*, 54/26-27). In this role the philosopher is simply a toy of kings, a kept curiosity like the dwarves at the court of Philip IV in the paintings of Velasquez.

In his answer Raphael demonstrates that he is moved by neither of these reasons. He has no desire for possessions. And the interests of his family have been reasonably looked after since he has already given them all his wealth (55/23-31). Peter, dismissing as mere words the question of whether his proposal involves service or servitude (55/32-33),[30] holds on to his point, but now with a subtle change. He reverses the stress of his former statement insisting first on the "profitable contribution" (*conducere*, 54/31) a philosopher can bring to the commonwealth. His own advancement to a happier condition is now only a secondary concern (55/35-39). The main gain is for others and the private good is no longer wealth, which Raphael clearly did not want, but the honour and power he would acquire.

Raphael refuses these as well (57/1-6). How could his own condition be made better when, in order to gain status and power, he would have to toady to the king? He has pointed out that these gains can only be had at the cost of entering into servitude to kings, which is not the role of a freeman. In any event, he will not be missed at court where there are so many who are willing to pay this price. In these exchanges Giles has drawn Raphael out and established that he is not moved in any degree by the desire for riches on the one hand or for power and glory on the other.

More now enters the conversation and makes this conclusion explicit (57/7-21). From it he draws two corollaries. The first is that if Raphael wants neither riches nor glory he is, on this account, not the opposite of the king but his equal. Thus he says, "Assuredly, I reverence and look up to a man of your mind no whit less than to any of those who are most high and mighty" (i.e., kings or royal counsellors—57/8-10). Secondly, he cites this as the reason for judging that Raphael has a "generous and truly philosophic spirit" (57/11). Not only does he have the learning and experience (57/18-21) of a philosopher but, in refusing to use these for worldly gain—in the manner of the ancient Sophists—he reveals a Socratic soul which is concerned above all else with the truth.

Raphael however has not properly answered Giles' suggestion that he should enter the service of a king for the good of the commonwealth. More now makes the point strongly and urges him to do so not for any external end but because his philosophical spirit, if it is to be true to itself, demands that he "apply [his] talent and industry to the public interest, even if it involves some personal disadvantages" (57/12-13). This is simply a restatement of the Platonic argument that in an ideal republic the true philosopher must use his knowledge to guide the state and cannot simply remain in the private contemplation of the Good (*Republic* 519c-521b). More suggests that the best way for Raphael to do this is to make himself "councilor to some great monarch and make him follow, as I am sure you will, straightforward and honourable courses" (57/15-16). More argues that there is "no more fruitful way" (56/12) and Raphael counters that, in the actual situation of Europe, he is altogether mistaken.

Like Raphael, Plato had argued that the best thing for a philosopher in an unjust state was to stay out of public life (*Apology* 31d-32a; *Republic* 496d,e). His own experience in trying to guide the tyrants of Syracuse, Dionysius I and II, to reform themselves and establish his republic had so convinced him of the impossibility of the venture that, when later the Arcadians and Thebans invited him to be the legislator of Megalopolis, a city they were founding, he refused when he discovered that they were opposed to the equality of possessions.[31] There is however an important difference between Raphael's position which, on this matter, I take to be identical with that of More (the author), and that of Plato on the one hand and More (the character) on the other. Plato taught that a philosopher could only benefit the commonwealth by his advice if he were "fortunate" enough to live in a state which was "adapted to his nature" (*Republic* 497a)—i.e., which was both capable and desirous of being guided by him. He thought that the practical realization of this possibility could only lie in some happy chance that would compel the philosopher to rule and the citizens to be ruled by him, or with the gods who might inspire in some actual ruler a genuine passion for philosophy (499b,c)—but he recognized that both of these things (chance and divine inspiration) were, by definition, beyond human capacities to engineer or control in any practical sense. Thus, as I will argue, his discussion of the ideal republic is just that—i.e., purely theoretical. More (the character) makes the generic mistake of European politics by supposing that Plato's theoretical prescriptions could be put into practice, and it is for this reason that he urges Raphael into the service of some actual, though admittedly corrupt, state—which Plato himself had not recommended. And Raphael, who agrees with Plato in maintaining that there is no place for a philosopher in the councils of any existing state, nevertheless differs from his teaching, *toto caelo*, in his confidence that it lies within human power to create and maintain the best commonwealth—after all, he had seen it for himself in Utopia which, he knew, depended neither on chance nor on divine inspiration. In this he agreed with the practical interests of More (the character) and so their argument is not about whether the highest and truest philosophy is practical or contemplative. Raphael never maintains that a true philosopher should not concern himself with the public interest even in an unjust state. Indeed, in his case the contemplative life was the life he enjoyed in Utopia which he *left* for no other reason than "to make known that new world" (107/ 21-22)—i.e., to the old, for its practical amelioration. Both More and Raphael agree that the end of philosophy is the practical transformation of the world. Their disagreement is exclusively about the means proposed by More.[32]

Raphael introduces the discussion at Cardinal Morton's[33] to illustrate how the contemporary European situation is so structurally corrupt that it is impossible for a true philosopher to have any hearing when there is an inequality of class amongst the participants of a discussion where truth is sought. The talk at Morton's table was something every educated reader would recognize from his own experience. Unlike the councils of kings where decisions of war and peace were actually made, the conversation at Morton's was free and unconstrained in the sense that nothing turned on its outcome except the discovery of the truth. But all the guests, except Raphael himself, were interested solely in playing the parasite to the Cardinal whose friendliness they strove to win by flattery.[34] In his description of the Cardinal (59/19-61/6), Raphael makes it clear that Morton required no such thing. He says this explicitly where he tells us that he, Raphael, "dared to be free in expressing [his] opinions without reserve at the Cardinal's table" (65/15-16): there was no need to disguise the truth for this man.

Raphael's well-chosen example illustrates the impossibility of a true philosophical discussion where there is an inequality amongst the participants such as that between Morton, a spiritual and temporal lord, and the others.[35] Even when, by his whole demeanour, he shows his interest and desire in seeking the truth, his position compels the others to play the flatterer—i.e., those who can be, or imagine they can be, in any way affected by him—and this included everyone except the foreigner, Raphael himself, who was not under his rule.

In relating the details of the conversation Raphael stresses this point, for his own contribution was by "all... received with contempt" (81/ 21), until Morton seemed favourable to it. The stated reason for this contempt is simply that he was a foreigner—as the lawyer says when he replies to Raphael in these words: " 'Certainly sir,' he began, 'you have spoken well considering that you are but a stranger who could hear something of these matters rather than get an exact knowledge of them' " (71/22-24). This point has no colour of truth since it comes right after Raphael's detailed and knowledgeable account of the unique problems of the English caused by their wool industry (65/38-71/7). It is nothing but a specious way of dismissing Raphael's arguments—although it was one that was necessary to the lawyer as the only way of appearing to take Raphael's position into account. It could not be considered for its own merits by a man whose speech and thoughts were constrained by his real or imagined dependence on the Cardinal. Raphael could not be heard by such men just because he alone, being a foreigner, was free to look to the truth while the others thought they had to look to the Cardinal. That they were mistaken makes no difference. In principle their inequality and dependence left them unfit for disinterested inquiry.

The farce between the scoffer and the too-serious friar which Raphael tells at the end of the Morton episode (81/23-85/38) makes the same point in the strongest way.[36] Here his guests are shown to be so slavishly and senselessly bound to Morton's every gesture that, paying heed only to what they take as his approval, conveyed by a mere smile (83/14) at the amusing but idiotic remark of a "hanger-on" (*parasitus*, 80/23),[37] they mistake it as approbation of the scoffer's idea rather than his joke and begin to fall over themselves in affirming the wisdom of his foolish scheme (83/26-27; 85/34-36).[38] And likewise the friar, who was the butt of the joke, falls into contradicting himself once ("I am not angry you damned slave"—83/36-37),[39] and the Cardinal twice (85/3ff. and 85/15f.), in an emotional response (85/2) that pits him as unreasonably against the Cardinal as the others are unreasonably for him. Both responses, the positive approving flattery of the many and the negative anger of the friar, stem from the same unfree relation to the man in authority. None can conceive how they could consider the weightless remark of the joker for its intrinsic worth since they all see it only in relation to the way they suppose the Cardinal has taken it. The whole business is, as Raphael had said at the beginning, "quite absurd" (*ridicula*, 80/21).

All of this may be taken as illustrating the complete inability of such men to enter a philosophical discussion because they lack the requisite freedom and disinterestedness.[40] This is the first blow in Raphael's attack on the Platonic doctrine of the necessity of separating the three parts of the state (philosophers, guardians and craftsmen) as the ultimate source of an inequality which made it impossible to look for, let alone discover, the truth. At first blush this may seem rather far-fetched and no real criticism of Plato, whose whole position was that only those who were philosophers by nature and training should take part in such an inquiry in the first place. Plato would not have looked for anything useful from a philosophical discussion between philosophers, guardians and craftsmen because he considered each class simply as such—craftsmen were craftsmen and nothing more. In terms of the analogy he draws between these three classes and the three parts of the soul (*Republic*

435a,b) he would ask how anything but the absurd could issue from an inquiry in which, say, the nose was allowed to discourse on the nature of rational truth of which, by definition, it knew nothing. Abstractly considered Raphael might concede this—but his whole point, as the example illustrates, is that real men cannot usefully be considered simply as reason, spirit or appetite as such. The lawyer, for example, did have in his soul the origin of philosophical inquiry inasmuch as he did "wonder" (61/13) and was puzzled at the great number of thieves in spite of what he acknowledged as the best possible precautions against them. What prevented him from coming to an adequate answer to his question was not so much the want of reason in his soul as the actually institutionalized separation of the Platonic classes and the resulting inequality which so fettered his rational powers as to render them useless.

Modern commentators, who have not taken seriously the clues which suggest a profound link between the *Utopia* and the *Republic*, have been content to see in the relationship nothing more than general similarities or isolated phrases and ideas obviously borrowed from Plato. This has led them to overlook the more profound criticism of the Platonic teaching which can be seen in the content of Raphael's speeches at Morton's table. To understand this we must first have before ourselves the doctrine which More found in Plato's work. This may seen a long digression but our trouble will be paid back handsomely in the end.

When, in the second book of the *Republic*, Socrates begins the search for the nature of justice by determining to look first for its quality in states, he starts by asking what is the origin of a state (369a). The answer lies in the desire to provide for human needs which he lists as food, clothing and shelter (369c,d) in a situation where "we do not severally suffice for our own needs, but each of us lacks many things" (369b). This diversity of needs in each man, coupled with the fact that "more things are produced, and better and more easily, when one man performs one task according to his nature, at the right moment, and at leisure from other occupations" (370c), leads to the creation of a city or state. Socrates then goes on to consider the minimum of distinct occupations that are necessary if the city is to perform its function. In theory the smallest number is four. A farmer for food, a builder for shelter and a weaver and cobbler for clothing. But each of these, on the same principle of the efficient distribution of labour, will need a number of other trades to provide the implements of his occupation. Thus the farmer, for example, requires a smith if he is to have a good plow and a neatherd to look after his draught animals if he is not to be diverted from being a good farmer. The city grows as a result of this calculation beyond the original four—but not limitlessly. In fact, Socrates completes it with the following: herders (oxen, for transportation), neatherds (cattle, for plowing), shepherds (wool, for weaving), carpenters and smiths for tools, "and many similar craftsmen" (370d), shopkeepers (for the exchange of goods), wage-earners (for unskilled labour), and then, on the assumption that it is "practically impossible to establish a city in a region where it will not need imports" (370e),[41] haulers and/or seamen (to transport goods to other cities), traders (to deal with the merchandise), and an extra crew of farmers and craftsmen to provide an excess to pay for the imports. With some such list Socrates suggests that the state will have reached its full growth and would be complete (371c). We need not haggle about the details any more than Socrates, whose point is simply that in a limited community of this kind the natural needs of men can be fully met, and met in a properly human fashion—i.e., one that is consistent with man's nature as a rational animal.

This is the minimum *state*. Below it there are, of course, other forms of association: the familial and the tribal; but Socrates does not discuss these because in them there is, as yet, no *explicit* recognition of man's rationality. Where the link between men is fundamentally natural (blood and kinship), there a natural rather than a rational self-sufficiency is the goal. There the articulated rational control of nature found in Socrates' settled agricultural community is still submerged in the natural limitations of each family or tribe which can control nature only to the degree that nature immediately permits. In modern language this earlier form would be characterized as a nomadic hunter/gatherer society bound to move with the game and the berries. Here the same basic needs for food, clothing and shelter are met—but only in strict dependence on the immediate forms of nature (diet of meat, berries and nuts; clothing and shelter of skins; etc.) and subject to its vagaries (scarcity of game, drought, and so forth). In such associations reason's demand that man free himself from this immediate dependence has not yet found expression.

Socrates, on the other hand, begins with the first form of human association in which man's rational nature finds explicit recognition in the satisfaction of his animal needs. This is the minimal *city* or *state* (what More means when he speaks of being interested only in "nations living together in a *civilized* way," 53/34, emphasis mine)—as distinguished from a familial or tribal organization. These latter aim also at satisfying man's animal needs but they do so in a form that does not take explicit account of human rationality.

There are several things to note about Socrates' first state. On the one hand, while it is the most primitive and undeveloped imaginable, it is also the most strictly and uncompromisingly rational of all the states

Socrates will consider. This is why he says of it, "The *true state* I believe to be the one we have described—the healthy state as it were" (372e). Its absolute rationality is shown in its relation to the family. It can seem curious that in thinking of this city Socrates does not begin with the family as the most fundamental level of human association nor does he even find it necessary to mention families though it is clear that the citizens will have children. This is no oversight. The family is not mentioned because it is not presupposed as the basis of this city, nor is it required for its continuance. Children are required for its continuance, but these are only produced in strict conformity with the demands of the state since its citizens will not go "begetting offspring beyond their means lest they fall into poverty or war" (372c). Everything natural here, including even the sexual drive—the greatest and keenest of the appetites (see 430a)—is voluntarily submitted to the rational satisfaction of human needs.

On the other hand this is also the most perfectly natural of all the possible states Socrates considers in the *Republic*. This is the meaning of his second epithet in the passage we quoted above. "The true state I believe is the one we have described—the *healthy state*, as it were." The sense of this can be gathered from the fact that here there are neither laws nor government. This too is no oversight on Socrates' part. No law or objective rational standard can be expressed because these are still embodied in man himself—in the limits of his natural needs. These, and these alone, are all reason aims at. And since such needs are objectively limited by nature or, as we could just as well say, by divine institution, the law cannot be distinguished or separated from man's nature— indeed it is his nature. In the words of a later poet, such men are just not by constraint or laws but by their own choice and by holding to the customs of the ancient god.[42] Socrates illustrates this in the vegetarian diet of the people. There are no pigs in this city—i.e., domesticated animals raised for no purpose but their meat (373c). This is because man's dietary needs can be fully met with vegetables and cereals so there is no natural demand for the complication of first feeding to pigs the grain man could eat himself—only in order to eat the pigs in the end. Reason's ends are in this way wholly subordinated to the demands of nature and just because neither has any independence from the other it is hard to say if there is private property or communal ownership. In a sense both are true since the farmer's produce is *his* produce (371c) and yet he *shares* the fruit of his labours with all (369c)—but one could just as well say that in this state there is neither private property nor a communist system of ownership.

Socrates provides us with a wonderful description of this Arcadian paradise which is intended to evoke the golden age of man's lost inno- cence as sung by Hesiod.[43] This "original," "true" and "healthy" state is so important to understanding the *Utopia* that we should have the whole text before us. Socrates, having completed his description, asks Adimantus,

> Where, then, can justice and injustice be found in it? And along with which of the constitutents that we have considered do they come into the state?
>
> I cannot conceive, Socrates, he said, unless it be in some need that these very constitutents have of one another.
>
> Perhaps that is a good suggestion, said I. We must examine it and not hold back.
>
> First of all, then, let us consider what will be the manner of life of men thus provided. Will they not make bread and wine and garments and shoes? And they will build themselves houses and carry on their work in summer for the most part unclad and unshod and in winter clothed and shod sufficiently. And for their nourishment they will provide meal from their barley and flour from their wheat, and kneading and cooking these they will serve noble cakes and loaves on some arrangement of reeds or clean leaves. And, reclining on rustic beds strewed with byrony and myrtle, they will feast with their children, drinking of their wine thereto, garlanded and singing hymns to the gods in pleasant fellowship, not begetting offspring beyond their means lest they fall into poverty of war.
>
> Here Glaucon broke in. No relishes apparently, he said, for the men you describe as feasting.
>
> True, said I, I forgot that they will also have relishes—salt, of course, and olives and cheese, and onions and greens, the sort of things they boil in the country, they will boil up together. But for dessert we will serve them figs and chick-peas and beans, and they will toast myrtle berries and acorns before the fire, washing them down with moderate potations. And so, living in peace and health, they will probably die in old age and hand on a like life to their offspring. (371e-372d)

Socrates has located this Arcadian city at once beyond family and before government at a point where nature and reason are contained in a perfectly equal and balanced relationship. When he speaks of it as the true and healthy state he means that it is, theoretically, the form of human community that is proper and adequate to man's nature as both rational and animal. As such, though it is a paradise, it is not a stable one. Its harmony will be destroyed in the moment that either nature or reason fails to seek its limit in the other. And since, for each, this limit is external there is, in themselves, nothing to prevent such a disruption. If the side of nature fails to be restrained within the bound of reason the city will fall back into the tribal and familial. Socrates does not consider this because such a relapse can, in the end, only issue in the reestablishment of Arcadia. On the other hand, if reason should refuse to stay within the bounds dictated by the necessities of nature the Arcadians will be forced out of paradise not by falling back into the family but by falling forward, as it were, into the luxurious or fevered city. This is exactly where the argument leads us as Glaucon (speaking for the reader) remarks contemptuously that this Arcadian state is nothing more than a "city of pigs" (372d)—i.e., one that may be adequate to man's animal nature but which is not really so to his reason.

Socrates, feigning surprise that anyone would want any more when all his real needs have been met, asks what more he would have and is told, "What is customary. . . . They must recline on couches, I presume, if they are not to be uncomfortable, and dine from tables and have dishes and sweetmeats such as are now in use" (372d,e). Socrates agrees to consider Glaucon's suggestions because they correspond to the actual condition of human affairs, which was Glaucon's point in raising the matter, and because he thinks that by looking at such a city they may be able to achieve their purpose of discerning "the origin of justice and injustice in states" (372e). In Arcadia neither justice nor injustice was readily apparent because everything was held in such perfect balance (371e-372a).

The shape and nature of the city that can provide the extra things Glaucon wants is radically different from the first. Socrates is firm and clear in characterizing it. No longer a paradise, this is a "luxurious city" or a "fevered state" (372e) and it is to this condition that he turns his attention. The difference between this city and the first is that reason here has freed itself from the external limitation of serving only the "requirements of necessity" (373b). It now follows its own inner logic as far as it is able to go. For these men, which is to say for us who have fallen out of Arcadia, clothes and shoes alone—and then worn *only* in winter when they are a necessity (compare the Arcadian's summer wear, "unclad and unshod," 372b)—are no longer enough. They desire everything reason can think of to adorn and distinguish their clothes and shoes which, as we might say, must now be beautiful, coloured, embroidered and made especially for summer or winter, inside or out, for work or for play. The satisfaction of these and such like demands, which are made by man's rational powers in their independence from the necessities of nature, calls for a qualitative change from the first city.

Not only must this new community grow by the addition of all the extra luxury crafts and trades which Socrates lists (373b,c) but, because it aims to satisfy the unlimited desires the mind can conceive, will of necessity be brought into conflict with its neighbours. And this all the sooner if these neighbours also "abandon themselves to the unlimited acquisition of wealth, disregarding the limit set by our necessary wants" (373e). The inevitability of war leads to the demand for an army and thus the introduction of an entirely new class into the city, qualitatively different from all the trades and craftsmen listed before. These will be the guardians whose special nature and education occupies the rest of

Socrates' inquiries. The function of this class is to keep the peace internally and wage war externally (415d). Some such class must be brought into the new city to regulate and preserve the unrestricted nature of the appetites when these are both defined and satisfied by reason operating beyond the limits of natural necessity. Otherwise each, having no *natural* limitation, is in potential conflict with all the others and indeed with everything else in the world.

In Socrates' account the distinguishing characteristic of this class is its θυμός (*thumos*, 375b). This word is commonly translated into English as "high-spiritedness"—the "high" bringing out the meaning of vehement passion in a good sense and is thus the equivalent of "courage." This is perfectly correct insofar as Plato intends to specify courage as the chief characteristic which must be present in the warrior class whose function is to protect the city. But *thumos* is more basically "soul" or "spirit" in the sense of its root θύω, "to rage or seethe"—i.e., the strong feeling and passion of the soul which can be both "courage" or "anger, wrath."[44] Its closest Latin equivalents are *anima* and *animus*.[45] This equivalence will be important when we turn back to More.

Socrates treats these guardians on exactly the same principle as he treated the other occupations—i.e., that each was best done by those who could tend to it exclusively. He asks what it is that makes a man capable of being a soldier where the end of the occupation is essentially an unnatural death from which one is only accidentally reprieved by times of peace or luck in war (386a-387d). This is the opposite of all the crafts and trades whose end is rather life and the satisfaction and preservation of the appetites—and in which an unnatural death would be purely accidental as, for example, if a farmer died from stumbling under his oxen. The answer Socrates gives is *thumos*, pointing to that element in the soul by which a person can oppose his immediate desires (self-preservation and the enjoyment of the appetites) and devote himself to a universal goal (subjectively, honour; objectively, the preservation of the city). It is not that *thumos* involves reason whereas the trades do not, since all the crafts, and especially those of the second city, use highly developed rational techniques. The difference is that in all of *them* reason is a servant of the appetites while with *thumos* the opposite is the case. Here passion is directed towards a rational or universal end for the sake of which a person will sacrifice his natural existence (see 368a-388d). Socrates did not mention *thumos* in the Arcadian city because it cannot appear where reason's goals are limited by nature's necessities. Once this restriction is removed, the liberated reason accounts for both the appearance of the new trades in the luxurious city and *thumos*—depending on whether it is directed towards the appetites or towards universal ends.

Socrates recognizes that a potency to move in either direction will be present in everyone (see for example the "noble lie" of the three metals,

414bff.), but he assumes that most, by their natural inclination, will move towards the satisfaction of the appetites and only a few to *thumos*. These latter alone have the capacity to be guardians of the city. But, in addition to high-spiritedness, they must also have a natural love of wisdom and learning so they can be trained and educated to use the spirited element only for the good of the city rather than turning against one another and against the citizens they are supposed to protect (375b-376c). And, of course, the latter is an ever-present danger because they are both stronger and prepared to die (416a,b). On such a class of rightly-educated guardians, the good government, happiness and liberty of this second (i.e., non-Arcadian) city entirely depend (421a).

This is what More understood Plato to be teaching and he puts the same doctrine word for word in the mouth of the pompous lawyer at Morton's table. This man functions as spokesman of the accepted and commonly held view. Raphael, in attacking the lawyer, attacks this fundamental premise of what is essential to a well-governed state and in doing so pits himself against an assumption in contemporary European thought that derived ultimately from Plato.

This lawyer had remarked with approbation that strict justice was everywhere dealt out to thieves—"twenty at a time being hanged on one gallows" (61/12-13)—and yet he wondered that though so few escaped execution the whole country was still infested with them. Raphael replies that it was no wonder since those who steal have no other means of getting a living. To this the lawyer answers, in strictly Platonic terms, that "we have... made sufficient provision for this situation. There are manual crafts. There is farming. They might maintain themselves by these pursuits if they did not voluntarily prefer to be rascals" (61/31-34). Raphael insists that this does not answer the problem which does not come from their refusal to be farmers and craftsmen but from the inevitable concern with war in any Platonically organized state. He first mentions the case of a farmer or craftsman who has been drafted[46] to fight in the service of his commonwealth, has lost a limb, is prevented thereby from practising his trade and is left with no other resource than to steal for a living. But these cases are rare because wars are only sporadic. His main concern is with what goes on in the state "every day" (63/4)—i.e., with its permanent concern with war even in times of peace.[47]

Here he directly opposes himself to the Platonic doctrine of the necessity of separating the guardian class for the good and safety of the city. There are, he says, a vast number of noblemen, and a greater number of their attendants, who are all idle in the sense of never having learned any trade so that, when dismissed from the service of their lord

because of their sickness or his death, they can find no way of living
except in thievery. As the soldier class they had been "wont in sword
and buckler to look down with a swaggering face on the whole
neighbourhood" (63/22-23)[48] with the result that even when compelled
by hunger they look down on a demotion to the lower class of farmers
and craftsmen. Such men are hardly "fit to render honest service to a
poor man with spade and hoe, for a scanty wage, and on frugal fare"
(63/24-25). Disdaining such ignoble employment themselves they are
rightly refused it by farmers and craftsmen to whom they can be of no
use.[49] The lawyer breaks in here with a reply that comes straight from
Plato.

> "But this," the fellow retorted, "is just the sort of man we ought to
> encourage most. On them, being men of a loftier and nobler spirit
> (*animi magis excelsi ac generosioris*) than craftsmen and farmers,
> depend the strength and sinews of our army when we have to wage
> war." (63/26-29)[50]

Raphael retorts that this is tantamount to saying that, for the sake of
war, the state should foster thieves since "robbers do not make the least
active soldiers, nor do soldiers make the most listless robbers, so well do
these two pursuits agree" (63/32-34). To sharpen and broaden his point
to other European countries he goes on to consider the case of France
where a standing army of mercenaries was kept which, in order to stay in
top form, must always find new wars, even if this means turning like
"wild beasts" (65/10) on those whom they are supposed to protect (see
63/36-65/14).[51] The individual thievery of the high-spirited men in the
English example is here transformed into a kind of general and
institutionalized thievery as this class, which is intended to protect the
city in the event of war, now actually becomes its cause in the pursuit of
its own separated interests.

As we have already seen, it is quite unfair to suggest that Plato did not
recognize this danger in the guardians. Precisely to prevent the high-
spirited element from turning like savage wolves on those sheep whom,
as guard-dogs, they were set to protect, he dealt at great length with their
education which was the "chief safeguard" (416b) against this evil
possibility and what a city could "do most to make them gentle to one
another and to their charges" (416c). Raphael however pays no attention to this aspect of the Platonic teaching but controverts it at the more
fundamental level where Plato asserts the necessity of separating the
guardian class from farmers and craftsmen. He denies that this is necessary even for the sake of war by noting that "not even the French
soldiers, assiduously trained in arms from infancy, can boast that they
have very often got the better of it face to face with your [English]
draftees" (65/16-18), whom he specifies as "town-bred craftsmen or
your rough clodhopper farmer" (65/19-20), i.e., Plato's lowest class. In

Raphael's account—which he clearly takes to be the real opinion of all present[52]—the lower classes themselves possess the required "high-spiritedness" (*animi vis*, 64/20) to fight in time of war, so there was no necessity for the state to maintain a separated guardian class in the Platonic fashion.

For Plato the entire well-being of the state and the whole prospect of there being justice in it depended on the identification, separation and training of this guardian class. For Raphael, who speaks here for More the author, the separation of a spirited class from the rest of the citizens is the chief cause of the ruin of the commonwealth and of the substitution of a showy justice for one that is really just or beneficial (71/10-11). The opposition between the two positions could not be more complete.

But Raphael has not finished for he goes on in his pithy and famous[53] account of the depredations of killer sheep[54] to show how, even in their pursuits which have nothing at all to do with war, the separated interests of the guardians—"noblemen, gentlemen, and even some abbots" (67/4)—have transformed these gentlest of animals into creatures who "devour human beings themselves and devastate and depopulate fields, houses and towns" (67/1-2). By turning out the tenant farmers and craftsmen from their ancient livings in order to raise sheep for the lucrative wool trade, these wolves in dog's clothing leave the ordinary citizen with no alternative but robbery and the likelihood of the gallows. Raphael concludes that no state can vaunt itself on its justice when, by its laws and the principle of its organization, it "first create[s] thieves and then become[s] the very agent of their punishment" (71/16-17). This is the condition in England and, by implication, in Europe generally because in Raphael's argument such a result is inevitable whenever there exists a separated guardian class according to the Platonic prescription. As the lawyer clearly shows, this was the conventional wisdom of the day. Against this Raphael has argued that in real life such a separated guardian class is both unnecessary for war and destructive in times of peace. For these reasons he urged its abolition leaving all as craftsmen and farmers.

At the base of this criticism of the Platonic position Raphael objects to its most fundamental presupposition which derives from the idea that it is helpful, in determining the nature of the best commonwealth, to treat man as having but one function. This was the premise on which Plato first developed the city—i.e., the rational division of labour according to which, "more things are produced and better and more easily when one man performs one task according to his nature, at the right moment, and at leisure from other occupations" (370c). Abstractly considered Raphael would concede Plato's point, but against Plato he argues that concrete, actually existing men are not such abstractions and cannot be usefully treated as such. In the real world, he points out, things are far different from Plato's abstract idealism when one *can* consider a craftsman simply *qua* craftsman. Raphael knew, and everyone in Europe knew with him, that farmers and craftsmen both could be, and were, drafted to fight—and that they did so successfully. In Platonic terms, this could only mean that they too had *thumos* and consequently this was not the exclusive possession of a separated class. This is the beginning of Raphael's effort to treat of man as a concrete integrated whole rather than, in the Platonic manner, according to the elements that can be abstractly distinguished in his soul.

Morton interrupts the conversation at this point to ask Raphael why he thinks theft should not be punished by death and what penalty would be better. Raphael's answer follows as a logical consequence from his rejection of a separated guardian class. The justice of contemporary Europe such as the lawyer praised is so abstract, so separated from the concrete situation that, in Raphael's words, "one may very well characterize this extreme justice as extreme wrong" (73/14). There is no equity in hanging a man "for taking a small bit of change" (73/23), unless one maintains that "this penalty is attached to the offence against justice and the breaking of the laws, [since it] hardly [pertains] to the money stolen" (73/12-13). Considered abstractly Raphael concedes that a breach of the law, any breach of the law, *is* a breach of the law but, as he says, justice based solely on this abstract principle is "more showy than really just or beneficial" (71/10-11). What he means is that real equity, a justice that is good and useful in and for this world must be measured in worldly terms and not according to an ideal Platonic form. By *this* standard, "not all the goods that fortune can bestow on us can be set in the scale against a man's life" (73/11-12). Thus it is "altogether unjust that a man should suffer the loss of his life for the loss of someone's money" (73/11-12).

The revolutionary aspect of Raphael's teaching can scarcely be over-emphasized although others in Europe as well as More were looking at things from a similar viewpoint—Machiavelli, for instance, throughout the *Prince*.[55] The new perspective, which is truly modern, can easily be seen by comparison with the still medieval view of Dante. In the *Inferno* thieves are placed much lower in Hell than are simple murderers, which is to say that Dante regarded theft as worse than murder. The reason is that Dante places the sins of men on a descending scale where the notes were determined not by worldly considerations alone but by the logic of the Christian faith. From this point of view simple murder or homicide (Ctos. xi-xii) was regarded as less culpable than theft (Ctos. xxiv-xxv) on both subjective and objective grounds. As a crime of violence, murder was thought to be instigated, in some part, by man's animal passions. Thus, as man was made by God in part an animal, so far, in God's eyes, was the use of beastly violence as a means of achieving his ends a mitigating factor. If in the violent act which is murder, man acts like a brute, it is because he *is* a brute in part—though he remains guilty all the same because as a *rational* animal his passions can and should be governed by reason.[56] On the other hand theft, which is, strictly considered, a crime of fraudulence against property rather than one of force against persons, does not *essentially* involve this brutish violent element and so we cannot point to it as an excuse.[57] Considered objectively as well, Dante understands thievery as more serious than murder because it is more subversive of the divinely instituted order of the human community. The thief, in confounding the distinction between "mine" and "thine" implicit in the rational ordering of property, harms the whole community *in its rational structure* and not merely its individual members. It is thus more damaging (because this latter is more fundamental to its proper order) than even the wholesale slaughter of individuals perpetrated by the likes of Alexander, Dionysius or Azzolino mentioned in the circle of violent tyrants and murderers.[58] Dante gives no clearer indication of the greater seriousness with which he regarded theft than by placing the monster Cacus in the lower circle of the thieves. He takes Cacus, the centaur of whom Vergil spoke, as one who "spilt abroad full many a time a lake of blood and death" (*Inferno* xxv,26). In other words his actions are specifically identified with those of the other brutal *murdering* centaurs—Chiron, Nessus and Pholus—whom he places in the circle of the violent in Canto xii. Nevertheless he is *not* found with them but, according to Dante's still medieval logic, in the circle he deserved for his worst deed, which was understood to be the *fraudulent* theft of Hercules' cattle (*lo furto che frodolente fece*, xxv,29).[59] Dante thinks Cacus deserves a lower place in Hell for the theft of a few cattle than the better position he would otherwise have merited if one had regard only to his bloodthirsty murders! And this is the creature whose cave, in Vergil's words, "reeked forever with fresh blood, while nailed up in vile pride on his cave doors were men's pale faces ghastly in decay" (*Aeneid* VIII, 261-63).[60] Such a view is far from the modern opinion of Raphael.

Raphael insists that the only true justice that does not merely look like justice superficially (i.e., abstractly), but is in reality "both just and beneficial" (*aut iustam aut utilem*, 70/8, comp. 61/18), must consider equity simply in worldly terms. It is from this standpoint, rather than Dante's, that no worldly goods "can be set in the scale against a man's life" (73/11). This now becomes the fundamental good on which all others depend. The result of this shift in perspective is that murder becomes the worst of crimes and thievery something far less serious. As Raphael says, "if equity has any meaning, there is no similarity or connection between the two cases ['of killing a man and robbing him of a coin' (73/19-20)]" (73/20-21). And, as a corollary, "it is altogether unjust that a man should suffer the loss of his life for the loss of someone's money" (73/9-10). With this position More introduces a fully modern view of the matter.

Anticipating objections of two kinds, both from the side of *justitia* (or, as one might say, from the side of the Church) and from a consideration of *utilitas* (the state), Raphael goes on to defend his position by answering each out of its own logic. Against those who say that, for the sake of the governance of men's wickedness, God has permitted human legislators to punish such like wrongdoers with death,[61] he simply places the Biblical injunction "Thou shalt not kill" (73/22).[62] That is, to those Christians who claim divine justification for the use of capital punishment, he answers out of Christian Scripture by pointing out that if human law can exempt the state from the obligation of the commandment, "without any precedent set by God . . . will not the law of God be valid only so far as the law of man permits?" (73/31 . . . 33-34). This makes it clear that men who claim divine approbation for this practice can only do so by flying against the direct revelation of the divine will as set out in the highest authority of the Christian religion. Furthermore, if they should try to argue that the commandment against killing comes from the Old Testament (in the Ten Commandments) and has been superseded by the New he asks whether any Christian wants to maintain that whereas the law of Moses only "punished theft by fine and not by death" (73/39), the new dispensation of God's mercy in Christ actually demands the harsher penalty! (see 73/37-75/3). The answer implied in this rhetorical question is "No."

On the other hand, as against the secular defence of capital punishment for such crimes—that it is necessary or useful to the public good—he answers with the time-honoured argument that the contrary is the case since a thief might as well murder the man whom he robs because he cannot suffer any worse penalty and has "greater hope of covering up the crime if he leaves no one left to tell the tale" (75/12-13).[63] Raphael has thus argued that an accurate analysis of the English policy will show that it can be justified neither on religious grounds nor on the grounds of expediency. This part of his answer is complete.

As to the second of Morton's queries—about what would be a better form of punishment—Raphael answers, in accord with his main point that true justice must be considered solely in the context of the actual world, by citing examples rather than by a rational deduction from ideal principles. This is the new form of philosophy. He begins by saying, "in my judgement it is much easier to find a better [form of punishment for thieves] than a worse" (75/17-18). His inquiry will not move from the fixed point of any ideal good but rather from an actually existing evil which is the current English policy. It is the very opposite of Plato's method. Raphael begins by citing the practice of the Romans on the ground that they will be acknowledged by all as those who, in the whole course of human history, were the most successful at "managing the commonwealth" (75/20).[64] With this in mind he asks,

> Why should we doubt that a good way of punishing crimes is the one which we know long found favor of old with the Romans, the greatest experts (*peritissimis*) in managing the commonwealth? When men were convicted of atrocious crimes [as opposed to the slender ones which bring the death penalty in Europe] they condemned them for life to stone quarries and to digging in metal mines, and kept them constantly in chains. (75/18-23)

The key word is *peritissimis*, "most expert." Raphael insists that queries of this sort must be answered on the basis of a knowledge that derives from experience in the world (*peritia*). They cannot be answered usefully or justly from an abstract or ideal knowledge of the question, which is the whole direction of the argument in the *Republic*. There a fixed and stable knowledge or *scientia* is sought—over against opinion and experience—as the only true basis on which such judgements can be made.[65] The form of Raphael's argument is the contrary. If you want to know a better way of punishing theft than the method presently employed in England then, he asks, why not look at the practice of those who ran the best, largest and most long-lived commonwealth in history—or else show me that what worked for them is not suitable for England. Raphael however does not pause for an answer because, while the Romans provide an example of "a *good* way of punishing crimes" (emphasis mine), he thinks he has had experience of an even better way in the example of the Polylerites where, unlike the Romans, the aim of their penal system is justice for the victim (77/1-7), benefit for the state (77/15-29), *and* the eventual reform of the criminal (79/11-14, 32-37). We should note the important point that the possibility of improvement and progress—which Raphael assumes in his search for a better way— belongs to the method of modern philosophy. This is because it does not seek ideal and immutable answers in the Platonic fashion—from which actual solutions can only decline—but looks for them in the sensible world where the whole is never present at once and where, consequently, there is always the possibility of finding a better way. This is just what is emphasized in Giles' *Tetrastichon*—the four-line poem he "added" to More's book (23/25).

> Utopos, my ruler, converted me, formerly not an island, into an island. Alone of all lands, without the aid of abstract philosophy, I have represented for mortals the philosophical city. Ungrudgingly do I share my benefits with others; undemurringly do I adopt whatever is better from others. (19/21-26)

The Polylerites mark the first irruption into the text of what an educated reader would understand as a purely imaginative and fictional excursion.[66] All the other places and characters so far encountered are modelled on real life and are recognizable as such. The Polylerites are not, no more than are the Achorians (89/33ff.), the Macarians (97/16ff.) or the Utopians (Book II). More weaves them into the text with a host of details to give verisimilitude to these places and to put them on a par with the real world of Europe. But he does so in the firm belief that the educated humanist will easily recognize the fiction—if only, as he jokingly says in his second letter to Giles (251/4-21), by the clearly-made-up Greek names which he gives them.[67]

More's reason for using these imaginative examples follows directly from his chief contention that in such matters real justice must be sought in this world rather than in the intelligible world of Platonic ideas. Granted this premise, actual historical events (such as the Roman practice) form one pool of experience on which the inquirer can draw—but it is not the only one. The imagination forms an equally acceptable source of solutions provided only that the following two points are scrupulously observed. The first is that answers from this source must be given in sufficient detail to avoid becoming abstractions in the light of the actual conditions of the world. This is, in part, the reason for the details which Raphael mentions about the location, economy and polity, etc. of the Polylerites (75/24-39) and the other fictional peoples. Raphael does not aim at the general or universal but rather its opposite and he does so at the request of More, who shows that he has come to understand Raphael's method when he says at the end of Book I:

> I beg and beseech you, give us a description of the island [Utopia]. Do not be brief but set forth in order the terrain, the rivers, the cities, the inhabitants, the traditions, the customs, the laws, and, in fact, everything which you think we should like to know. And you must think we wish to know everything of which we are still ignorant. (109/21-26)

In other words More wants the details and the concrete particulars. The more of these he has, the easier it will be to make a judgement as to whether Utopia is the best commonwealth or not. This procedure is the reverse of the Platonic where the demand at the start of Book II of the *Republic* is just the contrary. Glaucon and Adimantus demand that Socrates exhibit the nature of justice and injustice in and of themselves, abstracted from the conditions of the world. Thus Adimantus, urging Socrates to a new inquiry, says:

> no one has ever [yet] censured injustice or commended justice otherwise than in respect of the repute, the honors, and the gifts that accrue from each [i.e., worldly conditions]. But what each one of them is in itself, by its own inherent force, when it is within the soul of the possessor and escapes the eyes of both gods and men, no one has ever

adequately set forth in poetry or prose— . . . . Do not merely show us by argument that justice is superior to injustice, but make it clear to us what each in and of itself does to its possessor, whereby the one is evil and the other good. But do away with the repute of both, as Glaucon urged [in the myth of the ring of Gyges 359b-361d]. For, unless you take away from either the true repute and attach to each the false, we shall say that it is not justice that you are praising, but the seeming. (366e-367e)

This is the identical charge which Raphael makes against the contemporary notions of Europe through the whole of Book I—but Plato makes it from the opposite side where the seeming is the embodied and the true, the ideal.

The second condition, which must be met if the imagination is to provide an adequate answer to such questions as the proper form of punishing thieves or the nature of the best commonwealth, is that experience alone must be the ultimate test of all solutions that derive from this source. All must be submitted to this court for their final verification. The enlightened Cardinal Morton recognizes this at once in his comment at the end of Raphael's account of the Polylerites. "It is not easy," he says, "to guess whether it would turn out well or ill inasmuch as *absolutely no experiment* has been made" (emphasis mine; 81/7-9). He even goes on to suggest a method of testing or trying in the real world the conclusions of Raphael's philosophizing, stating that "if success proved its usefulness, it would be right to make the system law" (81/12-13). In other words, the particular (an experiment) is to be made the basis of the universal (the law). In this respect also the modern philosophy, as advocated by More through Raphael, is poles apart from the Platonic. With More the ultimate and necessary test of any system depends on its being "proved" in experience whereas the opposite was the case with Plato whose purpose, as he says explicitly in the *Republic*, "was not to demonstrate the possibility of the realization of these ideals" (472c,d). Plato explains his intention immediately after this where Socrates asks:

Do you think, then, that he would be any the less a good painter, who, after portraying the pattern of the ideally beautiful man and omitting no touch required for the perfection of the picture, should not be able to prove that it is actually possible for such a man to exist?

Not I, by Zeus, [Glaucon] said.

Then were not we, as we say, trying to create in words the pattern of a good state?

Certainly.

Do you think, then, that our words are any the less well spoken if we find ourselves unable to prove that it is possible for a state to be governed in accordance with our words?

Of course not, he said.

That, then, said I [Socrates], is the truth of the matter. (472d,e)

And so it is, given Socrates' intention. But all the same, Socrates does go on, in order to "please" Glaucon and his other listeners, to show "how most probably and in what respect these things would most nearly be realized" (472e). He will do this provided they do not insist that he "must exhibit as realized in action precisely what we expounded in words" (473a). This granted, Socrates launches on the famous discussion of the necessity of a philosopher-king as the "smallest change that would bring a state to this [true and just] manner of government" (473b). This discussion concludes pages later with Socrates' statement that, "To affirm that either or both of these things cannot possibly come to pass [i.e., that a true philosopher *could not* become a ruler or that a genuine passion for philosophy *could not* take possession of the soul of a king] is, I say, quite unreasonable. Only in that case could we be justly ridiculed as uttering things as futile as daydreams are" (499c). Glaucon agrees and from this it might seem that Socrates has done what he said he would not do—i.e., that he has demonstrated the possibility of realizing these ideals—but his following speech shows the exact sense in which he means his words to be interpreted.

> If, then, the best philosophical natures have ever been constrained to take charge of the state in infinite time past, or now are in some barbaric region far beyond our ken, or shall hereafter be, we are prepared to maintain our contention that the constitution we have described has been, is, or will be realized when this philosophical Muse has taken control of the state. It is not a thing impossible to happen, nor are we speaking of impossibilities. That it is difficult we too admit. (499c,d)

In painting in words his ideal state, it was only essential to Plato's purpose to show that such a thing *could in principle* come into existence amongst men. This will be the case so long as there is no element of his ideal construction which depends on anything that lies beyond the capacities of human nature as defined. The discussion of the *Republic* would be a "futile daydream" and impossible in Plato's sense only if, for example, its realization required that men should be entirely self-sufficient or that all should be true philosophers—which, according to the premises of his argument, are impossible. Beyond guarding against logical errors of this sort he is quite unconcerned to show how his state can actually be realized in the world.[68] It is enough providing that his listeners agree that it could be, *given infinite time and place*.

As against contemporary interpreters who insist that Plato's discussion of the three classes and so forth is intended to describe an actual worldly state—as if Plato were writing all along from the modern standpoint of More[69]—More himself understands the thoroughly idealistic character of the *Republic* and finds in this idealism the ground of his objection to the Platonic philosophy. He demands that a true philosophy—one that is not merely a "painting in words"—must be directed towards the practical transformation of the world here and now. In this he perfectly expresses the new spirit and direction of modern philosophy over a century before René Descartes—generally conceded the title of "father of modern philosophy"—who said the same in his "Author's Letter" appended to the *Principles of Philosophy* (1644).[70]

For More, the ultimate and necessary test of whether a philosophy is merely a futile daydream or, as his character puts it, an "academic philosophy (*philosophia scholastica*)[71] which thinks everything is suitable to every place [i.e., which is unconcerned about the realities of time and place]" (99/12-13), is how it stands the test of experience. This means that it must be both provable and proven in the actual conditions of the world. Above all it must actually *work*. As he says to Raphael:

> there is another philosophy [than the academic/Platonic], more practical for statesmen [than daydreamers], which knows its stage, adapts itself to the play in hand [the real conditions of the world] and performs its role neatly and appropriately. This is the philosophy which you must employ. (99/13-16)

At the end of this speech More acknowledges that while Plato's style of philosophy may well be both true and appropriate in a theoretical sense, it neither has nor can have any practical relevance since it is in no way concerned with its actual realization in the world. He allows that, "In the private conversations of close friends this academic philosophy is not without its charm" (99/5-7) but, as merely speculative and dealing with purely ideal considerations, it can contribute nothing useful to the question until the distant day "when all men were good" which, as he says playfully, is "a situation which I do not expect for a great many years to come" (101/2-4).[72] On this account he dismisses it as irrelevant to the task at hand, which is to work a real improvement in the state starting from actually existing conditions.

The reader may well object that the "academic philosophy" against which More inveighs in these speeches is not an ideal Platonism but rather the very concrete examples of the Achorians and Macarians which Raphael had just mentioned. This is true. But More's point is that such examples, coming from another world, are so beyond the experience of Europe's kings that they are as irrelevant as the ideal world of the Platonic philosophy. Raphael's testy objection shows More the error of this assumption. He says, "If I would stick to the truth, I must needs speak in the manner I have described. To speak falsehoods, for all I know, may be the part of a philosopher [i.e., in the vulgar understanding of the day, and as Plato recommended in the myth of the noble lie— 414bff.] but it is certainly not for me" (101/7-9). In other words he challenges More (the character) to tell him he has not seen what he has seen with his own eyes or to show him why he should not say what he has experienced.

Beyond the fiction of the text More (the author) did not of course suppose that Raphael had ever seen the Polylerites, Achorians or Macarians any more than Utopia (= Nowhere) itself. But the genius of this interchange is that it establishes the cardinal difference between the role of imagination in Platonic and modern philosophy. Whereas Plato's images (craftsmen, guardians, philosopher-king, etc.) are directed towards the scientific discovery of an ideal intelligible reality and are indifferent to their actual realization in the sensible, Raphael's function as hypotheses in the modern sense of "science" or "knowledge" where the transition from hypothesis to knowledge or, as we can just as well say, from image to reality, must be accomplished by trial and error in time and space. In Platonism the proof or truth of the images is neither sought nor found in the sensible, but at the extreme other end of the Platonic "line" (509d ff.) in the eternal and purely intelligible Good. This is the *only* point in Plato's argument where the hypotheses are transformed into pure knowledge.[73] More and Raphael on the other hand agree that this transformation, and the knowledge they seek, must be sought in the sensible—the very place where Plato despaired of finding it. What the two moderns disagree about is whether Raphael's examples are so outlandish that they are, for all practical purposes such as counselling a king, as academic, ideal and irrelevant as Platonism itself. To More's charge, Raphael answers that,

> To persons who had made up their minds to go headlong by the opposite road, the man who beckons them back and points out dangers ahead can hardly be welcome. But, apart from this aspect, what did my speech contain that would not be appropriate or obligatory to have propounded everywhere? (101/19-23)

In Platonism those who are going "by the opposite road" are those who insist on looking for the truth in the sensible. With Raphael the opposite is the case. In this "appropriate" he asks More to show him what, in his suggestions, is merely ideal in the Platonic sense or, failing this (which More does not attempt), why he should disguise or alter such examples. After all, as he points out in what clinches the argument, "The greater part of [Christ's] teaching is far more different from the morals of mankind than was my discourse" (101/29-30). This brings the reader to the core of the matter. As a Christian, More had to acknowledge that if his advice to Raphael were followed and such examples could or should be altered to suit the desires of men then the whole Christian religion might be altered as well.[74] For why should the pattern and example of the true humanity which Christians had before them in Christ's life and teaching not also be altered, in More's programme—"like a rule of soft lead" (101/34)—to suit the habits and customs of men?[75] This was totally unacceptable to More and he conceded the point immediately. This we can judge from the fact that he raised no further objections on this score. It is thus precisely because Raphael is a Christian philosopher who seeks the *embodied, incarnate good* — and not, in Platonic fashion, the intelligible good — that he is *obliged* to speak as he does.

True Christians, as Raphael observes, are not free like "crafty preachers" (101/30) to bend the text of Scripture to suit their desires. They must rather obey the rules of exegesis laid down by the Church. Here Raphael would have in mind such long-established principles of interpretation as that (i) the literal sense is primary, (ii) the more obscure must be interpreted in the light of the less, and (iii) the famous maxim of Vincent of Lerins that only that is to be believed which has been held "everywhere, always and by all."[76] Such rules are the very opposite of the principles of ancient philosophical thought in its strictly scientific forms — as with Plato, Aristotle or Plotinus — and as distinguished from the "dogmatic" philosophy of the Sophists, Stoics, Sceptics and Epicureans. This philosophy, as we have seen in the *Republic*, (i) sought to discover the intelligible by moving away from the literal and the historical rather than towards it; (ii) it found the real and substantial truth — in Aristotle's formula (*Physics* I,i) — not in those (sensible) things that are more knowable and obvious to us but in the intelligibles that are clearer and more knowable in themselves; and (iii) while it started with the opinions of men it strove to move beyond them as having no necessary connection with the truth — as expressed in Adimantus' request to Socrates (quoted above, pp. 48-49) which is, as he says, the real starting point of the whole inquiry in the *Republic*. As against this ancient tradition Raphael has merely extended the principles of Scriptural interpretation beyond the boundaries of the Bible.

Modern philosophy and science arose in this moment when Christians began to apply to the world at large these same principles which they had been forced to develop, in the first instance, because of their unique belief that the absolute truth was to be found in the world. Christians believe that the immutable divine reason, or the Word of God — known to and discovered by the ancient philosophers (see the text from Augustine's *Confessions* VII,ix,13-15, referred to above, p. 7) — is incarnate in the man Jesus Christ. It was the incarnation of the truth, its existence in the world of time and space, that forced them to develop the logic of the sensible since, for them, the *fullness* of the divine truth was not to be found in the intelligible realm but in the sensible — in this man who lived in Palestine at the turn of the eras. What I mean by the logic of the sensible is that they had to discover and develop the rules which were necessary to arrive at a knowledge of *historical truth* because they alone held that the absolute, divine truth was not only intelligible but was also embodied in this world. This demand appeared first in the rules of

Scriptural interpretation. For, if the truth *was* incarnate at one certain moment (in Christ), then coming to a knowledge of it depended on a host of factors which had no status in ancient philosophy. All at once knowledge of the truth (i.e., Christ) *depended* on questions about the reliability of witnesses and their relative authority, the accuracy of the historical record, the relation of the literal to the allegorical, figurative or typological senses, the means of resolving apparent contradictions between authorities and such like problems. For a millennium and a half Christians had operated with these principles in relation to one moment in the world—namely, the Scriptural record of Christ's life and teachings. In the Renaissance they began to apply them to other parts of the world as well in the confidence that the same logic which had guided the exegesis of Scripture could lead to a resolution of other worldly questions.[77]

Raphael, speaking for More the author, demands the freedom of the modern scientist and philosopher to examine everything and suggest anything. He can claim this as his right, and as the only right thing to do, because he insists that his hypotheses can and must be submitted to the test of experience and tried by experiment. He would not have them judged against any other standard and this is the only court to which he will defer. He sees no need to bend the truth to the desires of men and thus adopts a position that is, if only in this respect, identical to Luther's demand that he be convicted out of *Scripture alone*—except in Raphael's case he says nothing will convince him except *experience alone*.

This is Platonism turned upside down. We can now understand the difference between the *Republic* and *Utopia* as this is expressed by More in the *Hexastichon* or "Six lines on the Island of Utopia by Anemolius, Poet Laureate, Nephew of Hythlodaeus by his Sister."

> The ancients called me Utopia or Nowhere because of my isolation. At present, however, I am a rival of Plato's republic, perhaps even a victor over it. The reason is that what he has delineated in words I alone have exhibited in men and resources and laws of surpassing excellence. Deservedly ought I to be called by the name of Eutopia or Happy Land. (21/4-9)

The same position is found in Giles' *Tetrastichon* (quoted above, p. 47).

Today's reader is perhaps inclined to the opinion that the *Utopia* is no less "words" than Plato's *Republic* since neither one ever got off the page to be realized in the world. This view comes from a failure to understand the *idealism* of Plato's argument by supposing that his teachings about the life and education of the guardians—the community of wives, the method of raising children, their civil and military practices and the rule of the philosopher-king (Books IV-V)—were intended by

Plato in the *literal* sense as prescriptions he hoped to put in practice rather than images leading to the discovery of intelligible truth. In relation to the *Utopia* on the other hand there is a failure to grasp its *realism* as we tend to ignore as a mere hypothesis all that has not been realized in history. Thus, were it not for the Russian revolution, we would doubtless view Marx's works in the same way as the *Utopia* and maintain that his position too was mere words. To do this is a mistake which obscures the subtle but very real difference between More and Plato and one that was essential to the eventual triumph of the position (More's) which we now take for granted.

More is very precise in the *Hexastichon* to specify the difference between his position and Plato's. The *Republic* is only "words" because it is—just as Plato intended—the drawing in words or "delineation"[78] of the ideal state without any effort made "to prove that it is actually possible for such [a state] to exist" (472c). More's, on the other hand, is the pattern of a state in which he has "exhibited" or "set forth" (*praesto*, 20/6) every concrete detail of its men and women, resources, and laws with the precise intention that it can actually be put into practice.

Plato intended the state he delineated in the *Republic* to be taken just like the picture of the artist in the analogy he gives us: that is, as an imaginary concretion or example (παράδειγμα, 472d5)—i.e., *painted* flesh, bones and hair, etc.—of a higher reality that has its true existence in a purely intelligible form. In Plato the paradigm is thus "lower" than the ideal reality of which it is the image in the sense of being closer to the sensible. It forms no part of his purpose to see this image embodied further in actual hair, bones and flesh, nor is this necessary provided that actual men can see their likeness in the image well enough to be led through it to the intelligible forms.

With More the function of his images (of the Polylerites, etc. and, especially, of the Utopians) is the exact opposite. They are not, in the Platonic sense, a condescension to the sensible—an accommodation to the difficulty most of us find in moving directly to the intelligible notion of justice apart from recognizable images from the sensible world—but are rather abstractions from the sensible in exactly the same way as is a blueprint. They are thus "higher" than the sensible reality they image in the sense of being more intellectual. It is no doubt for this reason as much as any other that More wrote the work in Latin—which confined it to an educated audience amongst whom would be the persons trained and accustomed to working in abstractions. Just as a blueprint is not accessible to everyone but only to the trained mind, so was *Utopia* directed to such an audience which included both the new order of humanists and the old, but equally educated, scholastics. And yet, like a blueprint, its purpose and end was solely to construct an edifice in bricks and mortar.[79] This then is the difference between his plan and Plato's. This is just the difference Raphael insists upon when he first mentions Utopia by contrasting it with Plato's republic[80] where he asks, "What if I told them of the kind of things which Plato creates (*fingit*) in his republic or which the Utopians actually put in practice (*faciunt*) in theirs?" (101/12-14). Both states are images—but the realities to which Plato's words aim are intelligible (*fingo* = "to form," i.e., words directed to the logical forms), while those to which More's words are directed are sensible concrete deeds (*facio* = "to make, do").

In all of this we are witness to the most exciting—though some will say, depressing[81]—transformation in the history of philosophy as it turned definitively from the contemplation of intelligible realities in the heavens to the construction of sensible reality on earth. If we may put Adams' happy turn of phrase to a slightly different use than he intended, this was the point at which "a historic cape of the mind was turned, one which divides the medieval [and, we can add, the ancient] from the modern world."[82]

II. More's Criticism of the Platonic Doctrine of the Philosopher/King

We now turn to Raphael's attack on the second pillar of the *Republic* in which he opposes the Platonic teaching that "commonwealths will finally be happy only if either philosophers become kings or kings turn to philosophy" (87/12-13; see *Republic* 473c,d; 499b,c; 501e; etc.). The occasion comes from More's urging Raphael to put his knowledge to the service of the state, impressed as he has been by Raphael's "wise and witty" (85/40-87/1) words[83] at Cardinal Morton's. These have only strengthened his original opinion (57/7-21) that it is the duty of the philosopher to advise the king (87/7-15).

Why does More persist in this after what Raphael has just described of the conversation at Morton's? After all, Raphael both began (57/22) and ended the account as an illustration of "what little regard courtiers would pay to me and my advice" (85/36-37). Is it the case, as Logan suggests, that Raphael takes More's continued urging "to mean that More espouses the blandly banal approach to the problem of counsel embodied in such works as [Erasmus'] *The Education of a Christian Prince*" (*Meaning*, p. 66)—where the best way to improve a state is by its wise men attempting to move the king to good ends by moral suasion. And does Hythloday simply assume, in consequence, "that More is a bit thickheaded . . . [so that he] launches into examples that make again the points about councilors and councils that he had already made'' (*ibid.*, p. 113)?[84]

Though plausible, this view fails on close scrutiny because it does not recognize the difference between the examples from the discussion at Cardinal Morton's table and the new ones Raphael goes on to produce in answer to More's query. Logan sees no difference between the two but there is an important one: the latter are all drawn from the councils of kings where *actual decisions of war and peace are being made*— "where great matters are being debated with great authority" (99/7-8). This is quite unlike everything that transpired at Morton's when no practical action was to be taken as a result of the argument.

More is not "thickheaded" nor does Raphael take him as such when, at the end of Raphael's first relation, he says, "Even now (*adhuc*), nevertheless (*caeterum*), I cannot change my mind but must needs think that, if you could persuade yourself not to shun the courts of kings, you could do the greatest good to the commonwealth by your advice" (87/7-10).

By the *adhuc* and *caeterum* More means to show that he has taken explicit account of Raphael's points so far. But, so far, Raphael has only argued that for the most part courtiers are neither intent upon, nor capable of, a disinterested investigation of the truth—and yet in doing this much he has also demonstrated that there are men like himself and Morton who *are* interested in discovering it. This is the side More now takes up in urging Raphael to the service of kings. He allows Raphael's point that such courtiers are no help in this inquiry, yet, where somehow or other there exists a genuine philosophical knowledge such as he is now convinced that Raphael possesses, he maintains that it has not been established why this knowledge, when it does exist, could not better the commonwealth by advising the actions of kings. Raphael agrees that this has not been shown because he now goes on to prove his own position by discussing the *new* case of what would happen if a true philosopher attempted to influence actual practice in some royal court.

When More urges Raphael to put his knowledge at the disposal of a king he does so in the following words. "Your favourite author, Plato, is of the opinion that commonwealths will finally be happy only if either philosophers become kings or kings turn to philosophy" (87/11-13). This is curious because so far Raphael has said nothing which in any way indicates that Plato is his favourite author.[85] How then did More (the character) deduce this? Since the author has given us no clue as to how his character came to this conclusion in the context of the morning's conversation, the answer must lie in the point we have already made. It is because Plato was the philosophical hero of More's circle of Renaissance Humanists that he unthinkingly assumes a close affinity with Plato in any man who possesses a genuine philosophical spirit. If More failed to give his readers any preparation for this conclusion in the discussion to this point it is amply provided in the sequel—and it is not a matter which Raphael disputes.

Nevertheless More (the character) and Raphael disagree about what they find in the *Republic*. We can see this because Raphael begins his refutation of More's position by quoting Plato approvingly—but in the opposite sense. "Plato was right in foreseeing that if kings *themselves* did not turn to philosophy they would never approve of the advice of real philosophers because they have been from their youth saturated and infected with wrong ideas" (87/19-22, emphasis mine).

The difference between More and Raphael comes to this. Both agree with Plato that if ever a true philosopher should come to the throne, or else if a king could come to a genuine interest in philosophy, then that state would have the best prospect of being both happy and well governed. Both also think that, practically speaking, the possibility of such a union lies in a "distant" (87/14) future when, as More puts it later, "all men will be good" (101/3). We have already seen how Plato is unconcerned with the question of whether his recommendations can be realized in practice since he is only interested to discover the ideal or theoretical nature of justice in the state and in the individual. As modern philosophers neither More nor Raphael have this end, and both want a practical solution. What they disagree about is the import of Plato's teaching when the question about justice is redefined in this sense.

More takes a position which grants the practical impossibility of engineering a union of philosophical knowledge with actual rule, yet proposes that, failing this, the closest achievable thing to the internal union of these two in one man (which he, Raphael and Plato all admit to be the most desirable) is if a true philosopher were to *counsel and advise* a real king. That is, if a philosopher cannot actually become a king (which is out of the question for Raphael), or if an actual king cannot truly take up philosophy (which More knows to be impossible in the real circumstances and conditions of the world), then the closest approximation that lies in men's power, and therefore the end to be sought, is for the philosopher to become a councillor to the king. This is not in any way what Plato advocated—for whom such an external union would have been entirely unsatisfactory for his *ideal* ends—but it is a serious suggestion on More's part about how Plato's goal could most nearly be realized in actual practice.

Raphael maintains that such an external union will be useless. He begins by noting that the advice More wants philosophers to offer to kings is already theirs for the taking in the form of "published books" (87/17)—but these do no good. The reason is that in practice one learns that the long acquaintance of any actual king with false ideas, which have become an ingrained habit supported and shared by the vast majority of councillors, is what makes it impossible for him to be moved by the advice of a true philosopher. To do so he would have first to overcome the lifelong weight of his bad habits and become equally confirmed in good ones. Yet this too is the work of a lifetime—which is just what has not been done. And it cannot be done by any philosopher in the course of a single, few or even many meetings where actual decisions of policy are being made for in this situation the philosopher has not the time to re-educate the king and his advisors. And the king, from his side, cannot suspend the affairs of the world and the necessity of making decisions for the years it will take to acquire a real philosophical culture—even supposing he wanted or was able to do so. Plato, Raphael notes, learned this "from his own experience" (87/22) in the miserable failure of his attempt to advise and educate Dionysius.[86]

But Plato was ancient history so, lest More claim the contemporary situation was different, Raphael goes on to cite the case of the privy council of the French king. This example, as many have noted, would have been easily recognizable as a factual description of the real intentions and methods of the French monarchy in the period.[87] In such a situation the real desire of the king, nurtured in him from his youth, was an irrational aggrandizement of his power beyond any limits that a true philosophical consideration of the state could support. Here the words of a philosopher, which must aim at the contrary, could only fall on deaf ears. The opposition is between the king's desire for "glory" (91/5), measured by the extent of his dominion, and, on the other hand, the true well-being of any commonwealth which, according to Raphael's philosophical consideration, must not be larger than what a "single man" (89/29) can govern well.

To illustrate these limits, Raphael introduces the Achorians, "who live on the mainland to the south-southeast of the island of Utopia" (89/33-34).[88] This case clearly demonstrates the necessary limitation on the size of a well-governed commonwealth. In this plausible example they began to suffer the introduction of the many evils Raphael lists (91/3-9) only because their king turned his attentions to foreign exploits and thus away from the interests of his own people. In its origin this war had no connection with the latter. It sprang solely from an *abstract* idea that the king was "rightful heir" (89/36), "by virtue of an old tie by marriage" (89/36-37), to the throne of another country. The Achorians learn to their grief that such a right, and the "little glory" (91/5) that accrues to their king in enforcing it, can only be bought at a price that is ruinous to *their* real and immediate well-being.

There are two points here. First and fundamentally there is the opposition between the interests of the citizens and the king's desire to enhance his glory. In Platonic terms this corresponds to the division of interests between the appetites, or the farmers and craftsmen, on the one hand,

and *thumos*, or the guardians, on the other. As the one seeks a rich life and the other a glorious death they are by nature opposed to each other. Raphael makes it clear that the Achorians themselves were not moved by the desire for glory—as if they really wanted the reflected glory that would be theirs as subjects of a powerful king in a large state. He makes this point when he notes that they realized "they were shedding their blood for the little glory *of someone else*" (91/5-6, emphasis mine). The last phrase shows the Achorians' recognition of the Platonic principle that glory is not and cannot be the proper end of the people viewed simply from the standpoint of their immediate interests. It is not theirs and they must abandon it as soon as it comes in conflict with their *real* concerns.

Following from this, the second point has to do with the maximum size of the kingdom. The Achorians learned from their adventure that this is essentially limited to those who, having a natural community of interest with them, are willing to accept the rule of their king.[89] Presumably one must think here of such natural affinities as geographic location, history, traditions, culture, language, economic interests and the like which, in spite of the old marriage tie, were not strong enough in their newly conquered subjects to suppress "the seeds of rebellion from within or of invasion from without [i.e., by those who had no quarrel with the Achorians themselves]" (89/39-91/1).

This unlikeness in the interests of the two countries is what divides the attention of the king even after he has achieved his "glory" and vindicated his "right" by defeating them. It also forced the Achorians to realize that, because of these differences, "they would have to fight constantly for them or against them" (91/2-3). Faced with this situation they put it to their king that "He could not keep both [countries] because there were too many of them [i.e., Achorians] to be ruled by half a king" (91/15-16). This means that when the Achorians' interests could not be identified with those of the conquered nation, it followed that they must either accept to be ruled by a king who can only have some part of their own good as his end or else find another who can make the interests of all Achorians his sole goal.

Raphael's idea of the maximum size of a commonwealth—which he identifies as being no larger than France, a country that is "almost too large to be governed well by a single man" (89/29)—has therefore less to do with the talent and capacities of the ruler than with the number and location of his subjects who can be thought to share such particular connections (i.e., a common language, culture, traditions, economy, etc.). This judgement can seem surprising when we recall Raphael's earlier dictum that the Romans were "the greatest experts in managing the commonwealth" (75/20). Their empire was far larger than the French and included peoples of widely differing languages, customs and interests.

More has made no mistake in putting these two statements in the mouth of Raphael. They are not contradictory but rather point out the different kinds of rule More understood to be appropriate to antiquity on the one hand and to the modern situation on the other. That is, More's educated readers would easily concede that the Romans were the greatest experts in managing the commonwealth—where the purpose of rule was understood to be nothing other than an abstract unification of diverse peoples. The Romans managed this better than any and they did so by recognizing a common rationality in all men in virtue of which all could be brought under a single rational order—expressed in Roman law. The success of this principle, which led ultimately to the extension of Roman citizenship to all freeborn males in the empire (under Caracalla, in 212 A.D.),[90] certainly united the world but, aside from this one point of contact in an abstract reason, the Roman system had absolutely no interest in the concrete content or particular welfare of the peoples they united under their rule.

Indeed, the utter indifference of Rome to the particular interests of its subjects—so long as they obeyed the Roman law—constituted the second "principle" of their rule and was on the whole as scrupulously observed as was the law itself. It had to be—for both elements were necessary to Rome's universal dominion which was based first, on an absolute, soulless and heartless insistence on the law[91] and secondly on an equally strict indifference towards everything else—all that, in Juno's phrase, was "not covered by any law of destiny (*fatum*)" (*Aeneid* XII, 819). The one side is enshrined in that long list of heroes of the Republic from Junius Brutus and Lucretia to Marcus Regulus and Cato the Younger who, without flinching, preferred the law above all other things.[92] On the other side stands Rome's unrivalled ability to tolerate intact a countless host of outlandish deities, customs and traditions which she could welcome into the city and adopt with enthusiasm providing only that they did not conflict with her laws which gave the widest scope to the free expression of every conceivable particularity.[93] Both sides are present from the earliest days of the Republic in the standard formula which Rome imposed on her defeated enemies. They could continue to have their own municipal government, traditions and deities but must have the same friends and the same enemies as Rome.[94] The definitive poetic statement of the relation of these two sides is found in the terms of the reconciliation between Jupiter (who speaks for the primacy of *fatum* and the divine rational law) and Juno (who seeks and is granted the right to preserve the particular differences of name, language and dress not "covered by any law of destiny") in the final book of the *Aeneid* (XII, 818-42).

As opposed to such a concept of rule which aims essentially at world dominion[95] and which the Romans so successfully achieved—giving concrete form to Jupiter's word that "To Romans I set no boundary in space or time but make the gift of empire without end" (*Aeneid* I, 278-79)[96]—More insists on its opposite. We have already seen how Raphael makes this point in his discussion of the Achorians and we can be pretty sure that More (the author) thought likewise because Utopia itself—which is his model of the best commonwealth—is limited to a similar size by the same considerations. It is roughly 500 miles by 200 miles (111/7-13), or, as the editors of the Yale edition point out, "roughly equivalent to the dimensions of Britain as conceived at the time."[97]

Where Rome sought an abstract union of all peoples and was, as a matter of principle, indifferent to their concrete interests, More has not the slightest interest in a world state unifying, in some sort, all the nations. Instead, Raphael (speaking for More) insists that the true aim of the king should be an active promotion of the concrete interests of his subjects (how they are fed, clothed and housed) and a complete indifference to extending his rule beyond the given limited and concrete affinities which constitute the natural unity of his people. This change in perspective accounts for the emergence of the modern European nation-states out of the unity of the Holy Roman Empire. The change had been developing for centuries and was largely complete by More's day.

Thus, Raphael, speaking as the quintessential modern philosopher, says he would have to advise the king that

> he had better look after his ancestral kingdom and make it as prosperous and flourishing as possible, love his subjects and be loved by them, live with them and rule them gently, and have no designs upon other kingdoms since what he already possessed was more than enough for him. (91/25-29)

Lest anyone doubt the intention of "flourishing and prosperous"—as if Raphael meant these words in the sense that a Roman, or European, emperor would give them, i.e., "famous and splendid"—he has only to recall his praise of the similar characteristics in the Polylerites who

> do not try to enlarge their territory and easily protect what they have from all aggression by their mountains and by the tribute paid to their overlord. Being completely free from militarism, they live a life *more comfortable than splendid and more happy than renowned or famous* for even their name, I think, is hardly known except to their immediate neighbours. (75/34-39, emphasis mine)

This is Rome turned on its head. More speaks against the idea of a world commonwealth which had its beginnings in Plato,[98] its realization in Rome and, in his own day, had come to an end in the bankruptcy of its medieval form, the Holy Roman Empire—though only to be replaced by the misguided imperial designs of the leading European states.[99]

Where the point of departure for Rome was in the recognition of the common rationality of mankind in virtue of which all men could be brought under a single rational order, More has argued, through Raphael, that this leads inevitably to a government which, while it may be both "famous and splendid,"[100] can only purchase these at the expense of ignoring the immediate and concrete interests of its citizens. The point is similar to that made by Raphael at Morton's, where the older notion ends in an insane pursuit of an abstract and showy justice that has no relation with the real situation in which men actually lead their lives. With a clear and prescient understanding of the future that, sooner or later, all European states were to accept, he correctly identifies the point of departure of the early modern commonwealth as the sensible needs of its citizens, which is the diametrical opposite of the ancient position. It is also, in principle, as indifferent to *its* ends—i.e., power, glory and dominion—as was Rome to the concrete content of her subject's lives.

Of course the appetites of man are every bit as universal as is his reason, in the sense that they too are common to all. It is on the basis of this universality that the contemporary idea of a single world state, capable of uniting different peoples, has reappeared in the form of those two vast empires of appetite—Russia and America—which dominate today's world. As the end products of the new concept of state which More defined in its beginnings, the reader may be inclined to think that More made a fundamental mistake about the limitations on its size. In a sense this is true. But More's error, like the similar one in Plato, does not come from his failure to grasp its essential nature but from an inability to foresee the course of its practical development. More, who stands about as far in time from the developed form of these empires as did Plato from the Roman, is not to be blamed for missing this any more than is Plato for failing to develop Rome's universal state out of *his* principles. More could ignore the universality of the appetites for exactly the same reason that the Greeks could ignore the universality of reason and suppose it to be their own peculiar possession.[101] In both cases the universal aspect was of no practical consequence. The Greeks looked out on a world in which they were in fact the only ones to have explicated man's reason through the development of philosophy. And More, living at the end of the Middle Ages, was acutely aware of the strong differences in vernaculars, histories and traditions that had been emerging in the European nations for centuries. By his day these had become so diverse and so firmly entrenched that, for all practical purposes, they constituted a variety of differing forms in which, to be sure, men sought the satisfaction of their appetites—but not interchangeably: the Frenchman, as we might say, preferring his wine and the German his beer.

The past 500 years have revealed new ways of fulfilling the appetites which can ignore these limits—either by attempting to make all things available to the choice of the people (America), or by trying to educate all citizens to choose no more than what the state can provide (Russia). As a result larger states than More ever contemplated have come into existence but it remains that they have done so in accordance with the fundamental principle he enunciated. He limited the commonwealth to that size which could best serve the appetites of man. The intervening period has brought in radical changes in the means of achieving this end but none in the end itself.

In the remainder of his answer to More (91/32-97/38) Raphael goes on to show how a philosopher's recommendations on the domestic affairs of a kingdom have no more possibility of being acted upon than does his advice on its foreign relations. His examples parallel those he used before. He starts with a case that is intended as a recognizable account of the current state of affairs in Europe. This time however he does not specify the country he has in mind ("Picture the councilors of *some king or other*," 91/32-33, emphasis mine). From this I take it that More thought his description could have fitted any court in Europe although if, as Ames and Surtz have argued, it "fits the machinations of Henry VII,"[102] perhaps he intended the English to be understood but without restricting his description to that country. Then, as against the corrupt practices of contemporary Europe, he gives us, in the imaginary example of the Macarians, another people "not very far distant from Utopia" (97/17),[103] the model of how a true state would handle the question just as he had done before with the Achorians. In both cases the proximity to Utopia is, of course, more than geographical.

In domestic affairs the difficulty which prevents a king from accepting the advice of a philosopher is the combination of the two Platonic positions Raphael has already criticized. He thus completes his argument by treating together what he had formerly treated separately. The problem arises on the one hand from the presumption that the ruler of a state is owed a living by its ordinary people. In Plato this doctrine arose from his original position that each person should "perform one task according to his nature at the right moment, and at leisure from other occupations" (*Republic* 370c; see also 395b,c). Having gone on to separate and distinguish the three classes of craftsmen/farmers, guardians and rulers, Plato concluded that the only proper contribution which the first class could make to their rule was in the provision of all things necessary to the living of the guardians and rulers so the latter could be left free to pursue their roles without distraction.

In the *Republic* such things are strictly limited to the necessities of food, clothing and shelter. Since the guardians and rulers *qua* guardians and rulers have no need of any more, all luxury beyond these is forbidden them and even these they must hold as much as possible in common, eating and living together and having no private property (see 416d-417b; 464b-d). Adimantus objects to Socrates that his arrangement will not make these men very happy,

> For the city really belongs to them and yet they get no enjoyment out of it as ordinary men do by owning lands and building fine big houses and providing them with suitable furniture and winning the favour of the gods by private sacrifices [like Cephalus] and entertaining guests and enjoying too those possessions which you just now spoke of, gold and silver and all that is customary for those who are expecting to be happy. (419a)

In his long reply which is found in the whole of Book IV and the first half of Book V (to 466d), Socrates answers from his strictly theoretical position by showing that, if only one holds to the ideal forms, his arrangement alone will secure the happiness both of the state as a whole (420b-421c) and of the guardians and rulers as individuals (466a-d). The point is conceded and immediately after this (at 466d) Socrates launches into the discussion of "the smallest change that would bring a state to this manner of government" (473c). This is if "either philosophers become kings in our states or those whom we now call our kings and rulers take to the pursuit of philosophy seriously and adequately" (473c,d).

We have already discussed how Plato is only concerned with the theoretical construction of an ideal city in thought. Raphael on the other hand is concerned with the practical construction of a city in this world and he maintains that in the absence of a real philosopher-king—who knows the Good and can guide the city to it—there is nothing to prevent the guardians, and above all the king, from abusing his power and demanding, as a right, not merely a living from his subjects but everything they possess beyond the bare essentials. This is the true Platonic order turned on its head for instead of sustenance for the rulers and wealth for the citizens, such a state aims at the most extreme luxury for the king and the barest sustenance for its citizens. The king's interest in amassing all the wealth of the kingdom in his own hands and his belief that he does this as a matter of right and justice is the exact counterpart in domestic affairs to his desire for unlimited dominion in foreign relations. There he sought to use force—masquerading under an abstract idea of right—to subject foreigners to his rule. Here he uses an equally abstract idea of justice—expressed in the *pure formalism* of his councillors' crafty suggestions (see 91/36-95/3)—to deprive his own subjects of any independence in resources or spirit which could stand against his own power and glory. So long as a king has no knowledge of the Good (i.e., so long as he is not a philosopher), he is bound to suppose that the good and safety of the state lie in his own power and glory—for if these should fail there would be nothing to prevent the insurrection and mutually destructive competition of the people (i.e., the appetites, in the Platonic idiom).[104] As Raphael states the assumption of this received wisdom,

It is much to the king's interest that the latter [the possessions of his people] be as little as possible, seeing that his safeguard lies in the fact that the people do not grow insolent with wealth and freedom. These things make them less patient to endure harsh and unjust commands, while, on the other hand, poverty and need blunt their spirits, make them patient, and take away from the oppressed the lofty spirit of rebellion. (95/4-9; cf. the discussion of the tyrant in *Republic* 566e-567a)

In Plato's theoretical state such rapaciousness was prevented by a philosopher-king. Raphael argues that where there is no actual philosopher-king (i.e., anywhere in Europe) then it is "both dishonourable and dangerous" (95/11) for a ruler to act in this way. In stating, to More and Giles, the answer he would have to give to the king and his councillors, Raphael draws directly on Plato's arguments in *Republic* VIII. There Plato discusses the degenerate forms of the city—i.e., the city without a philosopher-king—which are, in descending order, timocracy (or the rule of the guardians, who are without a knowledge of the Good but covetous of honour), oligarchy (the rule of the wealthy), democracy, and finally tyranny. Raphael accepts Plato's analysis completely but foreshortens the argument by treating only of the first and final forms.

In Plato the first degeneration of the city which was once ruled by a philosopher-king occurs when rule passes into the hands of the guardian class who have *thumos* but no knowledge of the Good. "The most conspicuous feature" of this group of warriors is their "contentiousness and covetousness of honor" (*Republic* 548c). In terms of their rule these characteristics translate into "a fierce secret lust for gold and silver" (548a). They take these from ordinary citizens both because they can and because, as they suppose, they have the right to them. They alone have the higher virtue of great-spiritedness and, being disdainful on the one hand of "farming and handicraft and money-making in general" (547d) and, on the other hand, being the "simple-minded type[s] who are better suited for war than for peace" (547d-548a) who "fear to admit clever men to office" (547d), they erect the peculiar virtues of their own class into the absolute good. As an actual illustration of this kind of state Plato refers to the Cretan or Spartan constitutions (see 544c). Such men appear to be ruled by honour but in fact, as Plato argues, their rule is the most dishonourable and shameful thing in the world. They were established and supported in order to protect the interests of the citizens and yet end up having

compromised on the plan of distributing and taking for themselves the lands and the houses, enslaving and subjecting as *perioeci*[105] and serfs their former friends and supporters, of whose freedom they had been the guardians, and occupying themselves with war and keeping watch over these subjects. (547b,c)

Earlier (in Book II) he had said of this,

It is surely the most monstrous and shameful thing in the world for the shepherds to breed the dogs who are to help them with their flocks in such wise and of such a nature that from indiscipline or hunger or some other evil condition the dogs themselves shall attack the sheep and injure them and be likened to wolves instead of dogs. (416a; cf. 345c-e)

Raphael repeats all of this by way of showing how such ends and means as the kings of Europe actually pursue are in reality "dishonourable" (95/11). He says:

Suppose I should show that they [the people] choose a king for their own sake and not for his—to be plain, that by his labour and effort they may live well and safe from injustice and wrong. For this very reason it belongs to the king to take more care for the welfare of his people than for his own, just as it is the duty of a shepherd, insofar as he is a shepherd, to feed his sheep rather than himself. (95/13-19)

In the rest of his reply he goes on to point out how such means and ends are also in reality "dangerous" (95/11) for the king—drawing his argument this time from Plato's account of tyranny as the lowest form of the city and the one towards which all the others inevitably decline. We need not lay out the details of this parallel as the reader can easily do so by comparing Raphael's speech (95/20-36) with the *Republic* (563e-569c; see also Book IX to 580c). Both agree that a people treated in this way are the most dangerous possible enemies of the king (*Utopia* 95/20-26; *Republic* 567b, 568d-569c), seeking nothing so much as the overthrow of their hated ruler and stopping at nothing to achieve this end. And the king, for his part, "would surely be better to resign his throne than to keep it by such means—means by which, though he retain the name of authority, he loses its majesty" (95/29-31). Raphael sums up this side of his argument in these words:

To be sure, to have a single person enjoy a life of pleasure and self-indulgence amid the groans and lamentations of all around him is to be the keeper,[106] not of a kingdom, but of a jail. In fine . . . he who cannot reform the lives of citizens in any other way than by depriving them of the good things of life must admit that he does not know how to rule free men. (95/37-96/4)[107]

This is the purest Platonism and, in his account of the inevitable evils that befall a state which is not governed by a philosopher-king, Raphael is in perfect accord with Plato. The great difference between them is that where Plato overcame these evils from his theoretical standpoint with the *concept* of the philosopher-king, Raphael says that, practically speaking, we neither have, nor is it in our power to make, such a being and must therefore find some other means of establishing a happy, well-governed commonwealth.[108] Where Plato turns to the education of the ruler through philosophy and the discovery of the intelligible and divine Good (*Republic* Books IV-VII) to achieve this end, Raphael moves in the opposite direction. We see this in the positive advice he proposes to offer the king about how he should handle his domestic affairs (see 97/5-14). There is nothing here about the knowledge of the Good but only the most intensely practical recommendations about the concrete steps any king (who is not also a philosopher) must take to overcome the danger and dishonour consequent on following the crooked advice which is all that can be expected of his dependent councillors. The same point is made again, though here raised to the level of a principle, in the imaginary state of the Macarians. These people have been saved from the uncertainty of finding a true philosopher-king by the device of an earlier ruler, "a very good king" (97/22), who imposed an external, practical and concrete limit on the king's rapacity in the form of a law which forbade the ruler to have more than a thousand pounds at a time. For Raphael, the salvation of the state does not lie in the person of a philosopher-king who would make good laws by consulting their eternal pattern laid up in the *heavens* but in laws made by ordinary men and women who have only to consult the simple requirements of *this world* to discover the principles, embedded in nature, that will make people good. His address therefore is not to the prince (as a *speculum principis*) but to the people and it reflects a fully modern conception: man-made law as the basis of the state.[109]

Such advice had no chance whatsoever of being heard or acted upon. It was destructive of the king's power and glory, and thus of the very basis of rule in actual European monarchies. Raphael ends this part of his argument with these words. "To sum it all up, if I tried to obtrude these and the like ideas on men strongly inclined to the opposite way of thinking, to what deaf ears should I tell the tale!" (97/35-38). This concludes Raphael's argument against More's contention that he, as a philosopher, ought to advise the policy of some king. More had advanced the suggestion on the grounds that it would be the closest way of approximating the rule of the Platonic philosopher-king and Raphael has refuted him out of Plato himself by showing how Plato both recognized and foresaw all the evils that would befall a commonwealth not ruled by one who was actually *both* philosopher *and* king. Raphael has shown how the external union of philosophical knowledge and kingly rule which More had proposed as a practical and achievable compromise is actually useless in the foreign and domestic affairs of any European nation. More (the character) accepts this conclusion as we can see from his reply, for it is at this point that he says,

"Deaf indeed without doubt," I agreed, "and, by heaven, I am not surprised. Neither, to tell the truth, do I think that such ideas should be thrust on people, or such advice given, as you are positive will never be listened to." (97/39-99/3)

More had begun by proposing that Raphael ought to offer his knowledge to some king in the belief that, by his advice, the philosopher could turn a bad king to better ways. As a result of Raphael's argument he now concedes that his suggestion would be ineffective in accomplishing this end in any direct sense. All he can do to salvage his hope at this point is to argue that while a philosopher can neither *directly* control the king nor determine policies he ought still to advise him in the hope of *indirectly* influencing his policy for the better:

by the indirect approach you must seek and strive to the best of your power to handle matters tactfully. What you cannot turn to good you must at least make as little bad as you can. For it is impossible that all should be well unless all men were good, a situation which I do not expect for a great many years to come! (99/38-101/4)

In this last sentence More presents his new suggestion as if it was what he had intended all along. This is where he distinguishes between an academic philosophy, which considers truth abstractly, and a practical philosophy which takes account of the real situation—where compromises must be made and the most one can hope for is to make as "little bad" what one cannot turn altogether to the good (97/39-101/4). This, he says, is all he ever recommended and in a sense this is correct. As we have observed several times, the character More is only interested in a *practical* solution to the political problems of Europe. But when his proposal is proven inadequate he pretends that he never meant it in what now appears as the naïve sense that a philosopher could really guide a king to good ends. Instead he says words to this effect: "I too am a man of the world and of course I know about the compromises that reality imposes. All along I only intended that the philosopher's duty was to try to make things as little bad as possible."

Hythloday's answer, as Logan justly observes, is "cold and curt" (*Meaning*, p. 114) and the interchange is one of the most electric in the work. For a few pages (from the bottom of 97 to 103/24) the usually friendly address of Raphael to More—*mi More*—is dropped.[110] The reason is clear since More is dissembling when he tries to hold on to his suggestion by saying that he only ever intended it in this very watered-down sense. Raphael could have recalled the words More himself used when he first urged him to serve a king: "This [serving the public interest] you can never do with as great profit as if you are councilor to some great monarch and *make* him follow, as I am sure you will, straightforward and honourable courses" (57/14-16, emphasis mine). This is clearly a very different thing than his new and pathetic aim for

Raphael who should now content himself with making things as little bad as he can.

Raphael, though indignant, does not contradict More with his own words. This would only harden him in an untenable position. Instead he points out the contradiction in another way which More can appreciate. This is the argument we have already discussed which culminates in the unacceptable conclusion that, by following More's advice, the teachings of Christ could be accommodated to men's corrupt desires like a rule of soft lead (see 101/5-36). This is coupled and completed in Raphael's answer with a close look at the very thing More says Raphael has ignored—i.e., the concrete situation. He points out that the "tactful," "indirect" approach which More now recommends amounts in reality to bending the truth to make it conform to what they have already agreed are the corrupt desires and practices of kings and councillors. In reality, where actual decisions are being made, to hold consistently to a position which opposes the majority amounts to having no voice at all. One can only become influential by joining the many. The alternatives, as Raphael states them, are clear.

> For I should hold either a different opinion, which would amount to having none at all, or else the same, and then I should, as Mitio says in Terrence, help their madness. As to that indirect approach of yours, I cannot see its relevancy; I mean your advice to use my endeavours, if all things cannot be made good, at least to handle them tactfully and, as far as one may, to make them as little bad as possible. At court there is no room for dissembling, nor may one shut one's eyes to things. One must openly approve the worst counsels and subscribe to the most ruinous decrees. He would be counted a spy and almost a traitor, who gives only faint praise to evil counsels. (101/38-103/15)

What makes all this true is the fact that in this situation—which is no abstract or academic discussion where one can reserve judgement—a decision *will* be made at the end of the day. In relation to this *decision*, there are only the two possibilities Raphael outlines: either one agrees and joins the majority who, according to the hypothesis, are wrong, or else one opposes them and is voted down. More does not attempt to deny any of this which means that he acknowledges its truth.[111] How could he do otherwise, for Raphael has shown that if a philosopher *must* compromise the truth in order to be an effective member of the royal council then More's original purpose in urging him to advise the king has been frustrated and contradicted. This is just what he says:

> If I would stick to the truth [the original reason for having the philosopher advise the king], I must needs speak in the manner I have described. To speak falsehoods, for all I know, may be the part of a philosopher [as More has implicitly recommended in his advice to use the "indirect method"], but it is certainly not for me. (101/7-9)

He concludes by pointing out, against More, that Plato himself taught the same thing:

> For this reason, Plato by a very fine comparison shows why philosophers are right in abstaining from the administration of the commonwealth. They observe the people rushing out into the streets and being soaked by constant showers and cannot induce them to go indoors and escape the rain. They know that, if they go out, they can do no good but will only get wet with the rest. Therefore, being content if they themselves are at least safe, they keep at home, since they cannot remedy the folly of others. (103/16-23, see *Republic* 496d-e)

The argument has now been brought to a certain end. Raphael has proven to More's satisfaction that where philosophy and rule cannot actually be united in a single person (as opposed to their theoretical union in the Platonic dialogue) then the obvious alternative of having a philosopher *advise* a king has no better prospect of working— regardless of whether he proceeds directly or indirectly. The case looks hopeless and More, by his silence, shows that he is at a loss as to how they can get out of this impasse. This is the point Raphael wanted to bring him to and this is the point to which More (the author) had to bring the reader by showing him the inadequacy of the traditional assumptions. Now at last the way is open for More, Giles, and the reader to entertain a radically new solution.

It comes, appropriately, from Raphael himself who returns now to his gracious form of address. He can do this because his listeners have, presumably, been purged of tendentious arguments and are ready and willing to receive a solution from without—their own resources having been exhausted and proven inadequate. At last Raphael turns the conversation to Utopia and its principle feature, the abolition of private property. He says,

> Yet surely, my dear More (*mi More*), to tell you candidly my heart's sentiments, it appears to me that whenever you have private property and all men measure things by cash values, there it is scarcely possible for a commonwealth to have justice and prosperity. (103/24-27)

As against the Platonic prescription for establishing a just and happy commonwealth—the separation of the three classes and the rule of a philosopher-king—which have been shown to be either destructive in practice or practically unachievable, Raphael now proposes that there *is* *a solution* to the political problem which can be realized and which will work. The answer lies in the essential characteristic of the Arcadian city where there was no private property and what each individual produced was as much for all the others as it was for himself. In the *Republic* Plato was forced away from this state by men's actual desire for luxuries beyond the necessities of nature. It was these unlimited desires which destroyed the unity and harmony of Arcadia and forced him to consider the luxurious city and it was in this context that, from his strictly theoretical point of view, the separation of the classes and the rule of the philosopher-king appeared as the only means of restoring justice.

Raphael contends that a practical solution can exist if "private property is utterly abolished" (105/20-21) but that "There is no hope, however, of a cure and a return to a healthy condition as long as each individual is master of his own property" (105/37-38).[112] Moreover, he attributes this doctrine to Plato himself who refused "to make laws for those who rejected that legislation which gave to all an equal share in all goods" (105/5-7). The Yale edition (p. 379, 104/5-6) refers to Diogenes Laertius as the source of this information about Plato. Diogenes says, "the Arcadians and Thebans, when they were founding Megalopolis, invited Plato to be their legislator; but . . . when he discovered that they were opposed to equality of possessions, he refused to go." We do not have to rely on Diogenes since the same position is contained in the *Laws* — the last dialogue Plato wrote, the only one from which Socrates (i.e., the philosopher) is absent, and the one which contains Plato's treatment of political questions from a practical rather than a theoretical point of view. There, Plato's position, placed in the mouth of the "Athenian," is that:

> The first-best society, then, that with the best constitution and code of law, is one where the old saying is most universally true of the whole society. I mean the saying that "friends' property is indeed common property." If there is now on earth, or ever should be, such a society — a community in womenfolk, in children, in all possessions whatsoever — if all means have been taken to eliminate everything we mean by the word *ownership* from life; if all possible means have been taken to make even what nature has made our *own* in some sense common property, I mean, if our eyes, ears, and hands seem to see, hear, act, in the common service; if, moreover, we all approve and condemn in perfect unison and derive pleasure and pain from the same sources — in a word, when the institutions of a society make it most utterly one, that is a criterion of their excellence than which no truer or better will ever be found. If there is anywhere such a city, with a number of gods, or sons of gods, for its inhabitants, they dwell there thus in all joyousness of life. Whence for the pattern of a constitution we should look to no other quarter, but cleave to this and strive to come as near to it as may be in our state. (V,739b-e)

In the *Laws*, as in the *Republic*, Plato regards this as a divine state which, while it could perhaps come about in a small-scale way somewhere or sometime by fortuitous circumstance and the assistance of some god, nevertheless lies beyond the power of ordinary men and women.[113] From ill-breeding and ill-education in all existing societies men make a demand for the absolute ownership of property—for holding what is theirs by a right which is good against all others—and from this they inevitably forfeit the possibility of living in the first-best state. Plato thought these actual conditions were insuperable and so he has the Athenian concentrate instead on what men *can* realize given these actual conditions—which is to say the "second-best" state that is the object of the inquiry in the *Laws*. Thus the Athenian says:

> Now if we are going to look for an exact realization of our scheme, as we have styled it, it will perhaps never be found, so long as there are private wives, children, and houses, and if each of us has his private belongings of all sorts. Still, if we can secure the second-best conditions, which we are now describing, we shall indeed come off well enough.

Raphael, on the contrary, knows that it *is* possible for men to live without private property, and thus in Plato's first-best state, because he has seen "the extremely wise and holy institutions of the Utopians" (103/32-33). At first More objects with the time-honoured argument that "Life cannot be satisfactory where all things are common" (107/5-6), citing (107/5-16):

> the traditional Aristotelico-Scholastic reasons against communism: (1) shirking of work, due to lack of personal incentive and to over-confidence in others' industry, and (2) continual bloodshed and rebellion when want pricks them, when no one can lawfully call anything his own, and when no official (since all are equal) can restrain them. (Yale ed., p. 382)

Raphael answers at once that he is not surprised that More thinks this way, "being a person who has no picture at all (*imago rei*) or else a false one, of the situation I mean" (107/17-18), and he goes on to reveal that he had lived amongst the Utopians for "more than five years" (107/20-21). The editors of the Yale edition remark on this text that

> Hythlodaeus' answer is practical, not theoretical. He points to the *res*, the reality: Utopia, a supremely successful communistic state. As a philosopher, he should have met More's objections on the theoretical level. A philosopher does not solve the problem of Achilles and the tortoise by walking (*solvitur ambulando*). (p. 382, n. 106/13)

This is surely wrong, not only for the general reason we discovered earlier about the radically new character of the modern philosophy, but also, in the context of this specific passage, because More (the character) does *not* bring this objection against Raphael. Rather, with Giles, he is by now both delighted and eager (*quaeso te atque obsecro*—108/19-20) to hear the account of Raphael's experiences in the most complete detail (see 109/21-26). He would not do this unless he now thought that Raphael's account could, in principle, provide an answer to the practical problem and this is just what he—and all of Europe—wanted: a truly practical answer to a desperately practical problem. He has been brought to this point by the argument of the first book which has shown that the effort to apply Plato's theoretical solution to practical political life is not the answer but the cause of Europe's political problems. The book ends with Raphael's promise to provide this account after lunch and the reader, by now as fully prepared as Giles and More, is as eager as they to hear the solution.

Notes to Commentary on Book I

1 Surtz, Yale ed., p. clvii. The same is noted by D. Baker-Smith, *Thomas More and Plato's Voyage*, Cardiff, University College Cardiff Press, 1978, p. 4, quoted in Logan, *Meaning*, p. 35.

2 *Republic* 327a-b. The goddess is identifed as Bendis at 354a.

3 See the *Republic* (330d,e), where Cephalus says that "The tales that are told of the world below and how the men who have done wrong here must pay the penalty there, though he may have laughed them down hitherto, they begin to torture his soul with doubt that there may be some truth in them."

4 Socrates' question about whether it is right to return a weapon one had borrowed from a friend in his right mind, when in the interim the lender becomes mad (331c), may seem to posit so rare an exception as to pose no significant threat to the rule. This is the sense in which Cephalus takes it since it does not detain him from going off to do his sacrifices—i.e., as presenting no practical obstacle to his understanding of what he must do to be just. The question is however the most fundamental that can be asked, because it shows that an individual only owes something in relation to reason and a rational order—the discovery of which becomes the aim of the whole inquiry.

There are a number of recent commentaries on the *Republic*—such as those of R. C. Cross and A. D. Woozley (*Plato's Republic, A Philosophical Commentary*, London, Macmillan, 1964), or N. P. White's *A Companion to Plato's Republic* (Indianapolis, Hackett, 1979)—which seek to interpret the work from the standpoint and concerns of contemporary Anglo-American philosophy with much talk of Plato's "philosophizing" and of the "valid" and "invalid" points he makes. Such works, I think, are more interesting for what they reveal about modern philosophy than for what they can teach us about Plato (as opposed, say, to the older commentaries of Jowett, Taylor, Burnet and Nettleship—to speak only of the British tradition) as their interest is solely in the parts or themes of the *Republic* which they find "philosophically important." Thus, for example, Cross and Woozley quite explicitly regard their work as "an introduction to philosophy [viz., modern British] via the *Republic*, rather than a specialized Platonic study" (Preface, p. v), and White is consulted in vain for help with Plato's introduction in the first book: "I urge readers of all kinds not to dwell too much on Book I of the *Republic*. It is an introduction and is not intended by Plato to be a complete, or even a fully cogent, treatment of the issues which it broaches (see 354a-c). In my experience, it is not even a good book to use in introductory courses in philosophy ... because it annoys students more than it stimulates their thoughts, and it convinces them that Plato and Socrates were dishonest" (p. 8). This may or may not be true, but it is surely going to be of little help in understanding Plato if we must start from the assumption that we are primarily dealing with a poorly-written introduction to a twentieth-century college course. Could it not be that the "annoyance" White reports is the very thing Plato thought necessary to arouse in his readers as a starting point for his inquiry? If this is lacking, as it is with Cephalus, there will be no discussion.

Readers who are interested in examining current continental thinking on Plato should consult H.-G. Gadamer's useful collection of essays in *Dialogue and Dialectic: Eight Hermeneutical Studies on Plato* (trans. P. Smith, New Haven, Yale University Press, 1980). Gadamer's work is set largely in the context of German scholarship. On the French side the work of V. Goldschmidt is especially helpful (*Platonisme et pensée contemporaine*, Paris, Aubier, éditions Montaigne, 1970).

5   Compare the contradiction between the first and last words of Polemarchus in his attempt to define justice at 331d-e and 335e.

6   I do not mean to suggest that More thought Plato's *kallipolis*, or good city, had *ever* been realized—and, much less, anywhere in sixteenth-century Europe—but rather, as the argument will show, that he understood European politics as fundamentally informed by a wrongheaded attempt to put Plato's ideal solutions into practice.

7   See the Yale ed., p. 296, 46/8-10, for Henry's military successes which stood behind the epithet *invictissimus*.

8   For an account of the commercial treaties governing the export of English wool to Flanders, dating from 1478, and of the immediate circumstances and personages involved on both sides of the negotiations in 1515, see E. Surtz, "St. Thomas More and his Utopian Embassy of 1515," *Catholic Historical Review*, 39 (1953), or the brief account in the Yale ed., p. 295, 46/8.

9   Surtz (*ibid.*) holds that the alliance or amity with France intended in the letter of the Duke of Suffolk (see J. S. Brewer et al., eds., *Letters and Papers, Foreign and Domestic, of the Reign of Henry VIII*, 21 vols., London, 1862-1932, Vol. 2, no. 204, p. 68, quoted in Surtz, "St. Thomas More," p. 277) was "probably that concluded with France on 25 March 1515 which arranged for the marriage of Charles with Madame Renée, second daughter of Louis XII and Anne de Bretagne" (*ibid.*, p. 277, n. 8).

10   Surtz (*ibid.*) writes, "The plan of the Netherlanders seems to have been to make delays until the conclusion of the treaty of amity and then to seize English goods on June 24, 1515, the date of the expiry of the prolongation of the intercourse." On the distinction between the two separate sets of negotiations between Henry and Charles—the one, the general amity or alliance, the other, the commercial treaty or intercourse, see *ibid.*, p. 279.

11   Brewer et al., *Letters and Papers*, Vol. 2, no. 204, p. 68, quoted in *ibid.*, p. 277.

12   The violent undertones in the setting of the *Republic* are suggested in its dramatic date, 414 B.C., which everyone in Athens would have recognized as placing it right after the failure of the Sicilian adventure when, in the midst of the Peloponnesian war, the public good was jeopardized for private ends. See also the Thracian marching contingent in honour of the goddess (327a) with its new linking of divine services and martial force and the fact that the goddess herself came from Thrace which, to the Greeks, was associated with a semi-barbarian violence at the fringes of Hellenic culture. See also the unwarranted rudeness of Polemarchus' servant (327b) and the gratuitous threat of violence, however playfully intended, in Polemarchus' first words to Socrates (327c). This undertone becomes explicit in the character and description of Thrasymachus later in the first book.

13   On the central place of the wool industry in the English economy, see More's scathing account of the damage done by enclosure at 65/38-71/21. Although written almost a century later (*c.* 1596), Shakespeare's *Merchant of Venice* deals with the same problem of finding the proper place and limit of the new mercantile spirit within the

state. The play is treated from this perspective in the thoughtful article of Paul Epstein, "Law and Subjective Freedom in the *Merchant of Venice*," *Dionysius*, 7 (1983), 49-72.

14 For the impending or actual ruin of the Flemish and Brabant towns and their dependence on English wool, see Surtz, "St. Thomas More," esp. pp. 287-88. He quotes the words of Themsecke, Provost of Cassel, who averred that if the negotiations failed to come to a satisfactory solution for the Netherlanders, the men of Bruges would "rage and be ready to an insurrection" (p. 288).

15 On More's intention to stress the new humanistic learning and spirit of George Themsecke and on the man himself, see *ibid.*, pp. 284, 296. On the similar interests of others involved in making the treaty on both sides, see *ibid.*, pp. 295-96. On Tunstal, with whom More had a "most intimate friendship," see the reference in the Yale ed., p. 296, 46/14. Tunstal was one of the leading English proponents of the new learning.

16 So Logan notes (*Meaning*, p. 33), referring back to Surtz.

17 On Socrates' refusal to depart from the truth throughout his career see *Apology* 31e-33a. He did the same at his trial though it cost him his life (see *Apology* 34b-35d, 38d,e). All these details of Socrates' life and character may be found in the *Apology* as well as elsewhere in the Platonic Dialogues. Consult, for instance, the index to *The Collected Dialogues* (ed. Hamilton and Cairns).

18 Although no one, so far as I know, has seen this strict identification of Raphael Hythlodaeus and Socrates, Logan (*Meaning*, pp. 35, 100), does suggest a "resemblance" between Raphael and other Platonic spokesmen: i.e., the "Eleatic Stranger" of the *Sophist* and *Statesman* and the "Old Athenian" of the *Laws*. Along with the commentators of the Yale ed. (p. 301, 48/31-32), I accept the etymology for Hythlodaeus suggested by Vossius (in Thomas More, *Opera*, ed. G. J. Vossius, Amsterdam, 1695-1701, Vol. 4, pp. 340-41). Numerous other suggestions for the etymology, sense and meaning of the name have been proposed: see the Yale ed., p. 301, 48/31-32. See also the suggestions in Lupton's edition of More's *Utopia* (*Utopia, The "Utopia" of Sir Thomas More*, ed. J. H. Lupton, Oxford, Clarendon Press, 1895, p. 27) and Elizabeth McCutcheon, "Thomas More, Raphael Hythlodaeus, and the Angel Raphael," *Studies in English Literature*, 9 (1969), 21-38.

19 See *Aeneid* V, 848-53, and VI, 351f. The Yale ed. is wrong in the suggestion that Raphael is distinguished from Palinurus because the latter was not a "wide-awake" type. It is true that he fell asleep at the helm and tumbled overboard to his death—but only because Neptune required his death as a sacrifice (V, 814-15) and because the god of sleep, Somnus, sprinkled on him the irresistible dew of Lethe (V, 843-60). Vergil calls Palinurus "guiltless" (*insoniti*, V, 841) and stresses his devotion to duty in noting that his grip on the tiller was so firm that when he was "thrown" (*proiecit*, V, 859) into the sea he broke off, in his sleeping grasp, a segment of the stern and steering oar (V, 858-59). This is not the action of a man who was derelict to duty.

20 See Samuel Eliot Morrison (*The European Discovery of America: The Southern Voyages A.D. 1492-1616*, New York, Oxford University Press, 1974, pp. 4-6) on the first voyages of discovery along the Atlantic coast of Africa (*c.* 1430) under the sponsorship of the Infante Dom Henrique (Prince Henry the Navigator).

21 He is used as such by Dante in the "Inferno," (*The Divine Comedy*, text with translation and commentary by Charles S. Singleton, Bollingen Series LXXX, Princeton, Princeton University Press, 1970-75, Cto. XXVI, 85f.), where he appears in a very low section of lower Hell as a counsellor of the fraud (from the medieval perspective) that one can arrive at the Earthly Paradise by the exploration and discovery of nature. This, of course, is the very thing that More, writing two centuries later, would counsel his fellow Christians to *do*. More, though vague about the exact location of Utopia (43/1-5), places it on an island in the southern hemisphere which was the traditional location of the Earthly Paradise from which Adam and Eve were

expelled (see Dante, "Purgatory," in *The Divine Comedy*, Cto. XXVIII, 91-96). Dante's Mount Purgatory, with the earthly Eden at its summit, is located opposite to Jerusalem in the southern hemisphere (see "Purgatory," Cto. IV, 67f.). On a modern globe this would place it in the South Pacific some 2,500 miles northwest of Christchurch, New Zealand. More did not want to *identify* his Utopia with Dante's Mount Purgatory—which was, in principle, for those in a state of Christian grace *on their way to Heaven* (see "Purgatory," Cto. I, 4-6). His Utopia is not, as such, a stage on the way to the heavenly city. More would agree with Dante that we are not able to get to *that* place by nature but only through grace (see "Purgatory," Cto. XXXf.). Yet he conceives of Utopia as the earthly version of that heavenly Jerusalem in which, unlike Dante, he thought that it was possible for us to live our entire lives because he was considering nature independently of grace. In this sense it is as like to Dante's Earthly Paradise as it can possibly be without being a moment in the way of grace that leads to heaven—and for this reason he locates it as near in geographical terms as it was close to that paradise in a spiritual sense. This is how I understand the curious phrase in which More gives its (southern) latitude *as a function* of the difference between life and manners in Utopia (uncorrupted) and Europe (corrupted): see 197/37-38 where Raphael says: "But in that new world, which is almost as far removed from ours by the equator as their life and character are different from ours." I think that More intended the difference in the geographical location of Mount Purgatory and Utopia to correspond, as antipodes, to the location of Jerusalem and London (the Yale ed. finds other connections between London and the chief city of Utopia, Amaurotum: see p. 392). On a modern map this places it at about the Antipodes Islands [*sic*!] belonging to New Zealand, some 500 miles to the southeast of Christchurch.

    G. B. Parks ("More's Utopia and Geography," *Journal of English and Germanic Philology*, 37 [1938], 224-36) comes to a similar conclusion though he deduces the longitude on the basis of such maps and information about the then-known parts of the world as More did or might have known. He finds that More placed Utopia in the South Pacific somewhere between Easter Island and Tasmania (pp. 230-31) in the only really unknown part of the globe (before Magellan's voyage) which was thought to be capable of supporting civilized life according to the classical theory that divided the earth into five zones—two polar (uninhabited), two temperate (inhabited) and one tropical (uninhabited); see Raphael's account at 53/3-20. Parks argues, convincingly I think, that More more or less disregarded Vespucci's account to stick to the classical medieval theory which supposed that the equatorial zone was for the most part desert with only savage inhabitants. He reconstructs Raphael's voyage thus: (i) Raphael was one of the twenty-four men left at Vespucci's fort in 1504 at 18 degrees south on the Atlantic coast of Brazil, (ii) More then imagines him travelling overland southwest from the fort through the desert that ought theoretically to be there—in spite of Vespucci's testimony to the contrary—to the shore of the Pacific, (iii) shipping a rather short distance to Utopia at about the meridian which, to the north, touched the coast of China, and (iv) finally, hopping from island to island in a southern archipelago—or perhaps overland since Utopia is only fifteen miles from the "continent" [of Asia?] (113/10)—back into known territory, at Taprobane (50/17 = Ceylon or, perhaps, Sumatra, near Malacca, Vespucci's original goal on his fourth voyage), thence to Calicut, the Portuguese port in southwest India, and finally back to Europe. As Parks points out, this makes Raphael "the first European to circumnavigate the globe, anticipating the followers of Magellan by perhaps a decade" (p. 226).

22 Amerigo Vespucci (1451-1512) was evidently, for More, the most widely known, widely travelled man of his time. His books are the *Mundus Novus*, Basle, 1505; repr., *Mundus novus: Letter to Lorenzo Pietro de Medici*, trans. G. T. Northup, Princeton, 1916; and *Quatuor Americi Vespucij navigationes*, St. Die, 1507; repr. in

The Cosmographiae Introductio of Martin Waldseemüller in Facsimile, Followed by the Four Voyages of Amerigo Vespucci, with their Translation into English, ed. C. G. Herbermann, trans. M. E. Cosenza, U.S. Catholic Historical Society Monograph 4, New York, 1907. The latter was described by More as being "now universally read of" (51/7): see also the Yale ed., p. 302, 50/5-6.

23 Circe tells Odysseus what precautions he must take to listen to the song of the Sirens because she knows that his curiosity will not let him pass the opportunity by. See *Odyssey* XII, 40f.

24 Scylla and the Laestrygones are examples drawn from the *Odyssey*; Caelano is from the *Aeneid*.

25 According to Diogenes Laertius (*Lives of Eminent Philosophers*, trans. R. D. Hicks, 2 vols., rev. ed., Loeb Classical Library, Cambridge, Mass., Harvard University Press, 1972, III, 6-7 and 18-24) Plato travelled to Megara to see Euclides, to the famous mathematician Theodorus in Cyrene, to the Pythagoreans of Tarentum in Italy, and thence to Egypt to those who interpreted the will of the gods. Later, he went three times to Sicily where, in Syracuse, he tried vainly to influence its tyrants, Dionysius I and II, to put his political schemes into practice.

26 Compare also Aristotle, *Metaphysics*, I,2,982b12.

27 See Yale ed., esp. pp. xix-xx.

28 The account in the Yale ed. (1965) is a modified form of what Hexter had first proposed in *More's "Utopia"* (1952). The argument had been anticipated in Hermann Oncken's introduction to Gerhard Ritter's German translation of *Utopia*, Berlin, 1922, pp. 11*-12*.

29 Like More, Plato recognized the great difficulty and danger which a philosopher would experience in attempting to explain the intelligible good, which he had seen in another world, to those who were still chained in the cave of this world (see *Republic* 516c-517a). In Plato's answer to this problem, force was required to get a philosopher to concern himself with the affairs of this world (519d) and to get those in the cave to consider anything other than the shadows which they took for reality (515c-e). As he did not know where such force might actually be found he acknowledged that the realization of his just state could only be brought about by good fortune or divine inspiration (497a). In a very real sense the argument of Book I of the *Utopia* performs the role of this force in the *Republic*—i.e., it is that which connects the two worlds. I maintain that More could only think this possible if, unlike Plato, he had the confidence that the two realms of reason and sensation were essentially one—and he had this confidence from the Christian position which maintained that God had done this much, and revealed it to us, in Christ.

30 In the sequel of Book I, Raphael shows exactly why it is not a matter of words but how, in the context of the political realities of Europe, it really is a form of *servitude* for a philosopher to counsel a king.

31 See Diogenes Laertius, *Lives*, III, 18-23. In the *Republic* Plato is clear "that there would always have to be resident in such a [true] state an element having the same conception of its constitution that (you) the lawgiver had in framing its laws" (497d). In other words a philosopher/king can do nothing on his own and unless this condition is met has no prospect of success. The Arcadians and Thebans failed this test in refusing to recognize the equality of possessions.

32 Logan (*Meaning*, *passim* but see esp. the references to *honestas* and *utilitas* in the Index) agrees with this but finds that the argument between Raphael and More is about whether *honestas* and *utilitas*, the moral and the expedient, are really one and the same so that the former can be made the basis of the latter and vice versa—which he claims is Raphael's position—or whether (More's position) they do not and cannot always be made to agree (p. 121). The difficulty with this approach is that if this really is what *Utopia* is about, then its "meaning" can only be the very tentative conclusion

Logan finds in it: Raphael is on the whole correct—*but not always* (see pp. 251-70). There is so much leeway in this uncertainty that Logan is forced in the end to say that on just this question of the identity of *honestas* and *utilitas*, it is "impossible" to tell what More thought or recommended (pp. 121-22).

This also explains why Logan sees the work as a version of what he calls the "best-commonwealth exercise" (p. 136) or "game" (p. 243) in which the real contribution and meaning of *Utopia* is not so much in its conclusion (indefinite and uncertain) but in its *method*—i.e., the creation of a model of the best commonwealth by which one can test all the possible permutations and combinations to see which produce the optimal results (see pp. 60-61, 104-105, 130). Logan himself seems embarrassed by the clearly unhistorical implication of this position. He writes, "Of course More did not think in terms of theoretical models. But the fact that this twentieth-century term so precisely fits the Polylerite example suggests that it is correct to regard the episode as embodying an anticipation of this powerful methodological concept" (pp. 65-66). Without intending it, Logan seems to end up with a position that has More "anticipating" developments centuries ahead of his time and thus might have the same charge of "appalling anachronism," which he levelled against Kautsky (p. 7), turned against himself.

33 Morton was More's mentor (87/2-4). For details of More's favourable opinion of the Cardinal, see Raphael's speech at 59/19-61/5 and the notes in the Yale ed., p. 314, 58/19. John Morton (1420?-1500) had become Henry VII's principal counsellor on his accession to the throne in 1485. He was made Archbishop of Canterbury in 1486, Lord Chancellor in 1487 and was created a Cardinal in 1493.

34 Raphael makes this point at the beginning of his speech about the episode at Morton's (57/31-36) and again at the end of it (85/27-38).

35 Raphael stresses the aspect of Morton's power as a ruler when he says, "The king [Henry VII] placed the greatest confidence in his advice, and the commonwealth seemed much to depend on him when I was there" (59/39-61/1).

36 Because it is so pertinent to More's argument, it does not seem correct to take at face value the statement that he wanted to take out this episode because of its bad Latinity (see the note in the Yale ed., p. 345, 80/21). I see this rather as a subtle joke against the pretentiousness of Brixius. More himself made no claims for the good Latinity of Utopia (see the letter to Giles, 38/9-15) though in part this was no doubt a conceit and convention of Renaissance Humanism (see Logan, *Meaning*, pp. 19-22). Raphael's thoughts about suppressing the episode stress that while "quite absurd" (81/24), it nevertheless "had some bearing on the matter in question" (81/25). This is the reason why More wrote it in the first place and his "hesitation" was only a means of sugar-coating a pill which he suspected (correctly) would offend some sensibilities by its vulgar "low-life" aspect.

37 "Hanger-on" is probably the best English translation of *parasitus*. For the derivation, see Yale ed., p. 345, 80/23. This man is also characterized as a *morionem* = "fool" (80/24) and a *scurra* = "scoffer" (82/28).

38 The idiocy of suggesting that beggars could be enrolled in monasteries is probably lost on today's readers to whom this might seem a good suggestion. More however would have understood that beggars, like all other men, were already free to join a monastery as an alternative to wandering about homeless and without resources. On the other hand the idea of forcing people into a Benedictine monastery was equally ridiculous because, as everyone knew, one could only enter the order voluntarily. On this point Benedict's *Rule* was both clear and strict in its requirements for lengthy and difficult testing of the novitiate's will to become a monk lest he come in under false assumptions.

39 I have loosely translated *furcifer* as "damned slave" to convey the sense intended by More—in line with the tone of the other names the friar called the scoffer. Literally

the word means a "gallows-rogue"—"used as a term of vituperation, usually of slaves" (C. T. Lewis and C. Short, *A Latin Dictionary*, Oxford, Clarendon Press, 1969).

40 See the note on this point in the Yale ed., p. 309, 56/1. In real life More was very conscious of this point as we may see from his speech as speaker or "Common Mouth" at the opening of Parliament on 18 April 1523 which Chambers quotes (*More*, pp. 202-203) and of which he says, "It is the first recorded plea [to the king] for freedom of speech in Parliament, as against an anticipatory request for pardon." Chambers is, I think, correct in seeing this as "epoch-making" (p. 201) and his account of the circumstances and of prior practice is excellent. More argues that unless the king ignores the inequality in their respective positions and grants the Commons the right to say what they think "freely and without doubt of your dreadful displeasure," their advice will be worth little. If anything further is needed to cinch this point we have only to recall that More died merely because, as counsellor to the king, he held, privately, an opinion which went against that of his king. There could be no useful discussion of the truth where, as Tudor statesmen could never forget, "The wrath of the King is Death" (see Chambers, *More*, pp. 244, 300).

41 This will not seem obvious until one recognizes that Socrates is thinking of an area of perhaps 100 square miles. It would be hard, anywhere in the world, let alone Greece, to find a place of this size where nature has provided all the requisites—trees, arable land, stone, fresh water, iron, temperate climate, etc.

42 So Vergil, in describing a similar primitive innocence (under the rule of Latinus), which he calls the Saturnian Golden Age: "Know that our Latins / Come of Saturn's race, that we are just— / Not by constraint or laws, but by our choice / And habit of our ancient god" (*Aeneid*, trans. Robert Fitzgerald, New York, Random House, 1983, p. 202: VII, 268-71).

43 See the fragment of Hesiod's *Works and Days*, quoted by Plato in *Cratylus*, 397c.

44 Plato derives θυμός from θύω in *Cratylus*, 419e; "rightly," in the estimate of H. G. Liddell and R. Scott (*A Greek-English Lexicon, with a Supplement*, Oxford, Clarendon Press, 1968, p. 810).

45 Liddell and Scott, *Abridged Greek-English Lexicon*, Oxford, Clarendon Press, 1966, art., θυμός.

46 That More is speaking of draftees is specified at 64/15 where they are called *evocati*.

47 See esp. 65/30-34 which sums up the discussion of the evils of separating the guardian class.

48 The editors of the Yale ed. (p. 318, 62/7-8) say that, in spite of the reference to "sword and buckler," More intends "household servants rather than liveried and feed retainers, whose obligation was only to 'ride and go' with their lord, 'defensibly arrayed,' and whose availability for private armies was a matter of concern and danger in the fifteenth century" (p. 319). The argument has shown that such *armed men* are just the ones More would have had in mind—i.e., the guardian class.

49 In the *Tempest* (III,1), Prospero tests Ferdinand's mettle and worth by his willingness to do such hard, "ignoble" work for the sake of Miranda. He has him move a pile of some thousands of logs. Written a century after *Utopia*, Shakespeare teaches here the same lesson. And Ferdinand, expressing the opinions of the nobility, shows both how little had changed since More's time: "I am, in my condition / A prince, Miranda; I do think, a king / . . . and would no more endure this wooden slavery than suffer / The flesh-fly blow my mouth"—and how much—for he ends by saying: "Hear my soul speak: / The very instant that I saw you, did / My heart fly to your service; there resides, / To make me slave to it; as for your sake / Am I this patient log-man" (ll. 59-67).

50 This "spirit" (*animus*) is the proper translation of Plato's θυμός (see Liddell and Scott, *Abridged Greek-English Lexicon*).

51 The quotation from Sallust (*Catiline Conspiracy*, 16, in *Sallust*, trans. J. C. Rolfe, Loeb Classical Library, rev. ed., Cambridge, Mass., Harvard University Press, 1931) likens the guardians to Catiline, the arch-villain of the Roman Republic, who attempted and was prepared to ruin the whole state for no other purpose than to satisfy his private ends. Augustine uses this same text for similar purposes in his *Confessions* (II,v,11).

52 There being no argument to the contrary and because he prefaces these remarks with the statement that he will not say too much on this score "for fear of seeming to flatter you barefacedly" (65/18).

53 See Yale ed., p. 326, 64/31, where Harpsfield is quoted as saying that, of the three points he notes as distinctive about the *Utopia*, one is that More has a "mervailous inopinable probleme of sheepe."

54 The reference is to the great movement known as "enclosure"—on which see the two notes in the Yale ed., at 64/31 (pp. 325, 326) and the other relevant notes in the following pages.

55 By the similarity of viewpoint between More and Machiavelli, I mean that both are intent on developing a state in which Christians could live, but which was also independent of any explicit and necessary relation to the Church. Granted this identity of purpose the interesting questions of the similarity and difference in what each man proposed as the solution lies, unfortunately, beyond the scope of this essay.

56 Dante gives us an image of the divided nature of man, whose animal or bestial nature lies at the root of this sin, in the monsters he sets as the demonic guardians and chastisers in this circle of Hell: i.e., the Minotaur and Centaurs who are half-man and half-beast—a human body with a bull's head; horses' bodies with human torso and head (see "Inferno," Cto. XII).

57 In Canto XI of the "Inferno," where Dante describes the logic of the arrangement of lower Hell, it can seem as if he places robbers amongst the circle of tyrants and murderers who were violent against their neighbours.

> Morte per forza e ferute dogliose
> nel prossimo di danno, e nel suo avere
> ruine, incendi e tollete dannoso;
> onde omicide e ciascun che mal fiere,
> guastatori e predon, tutti tormenta
> lo giron primo per diveres schiere. (34-39)

Predone is a "plunderer, robber or highwayman," but Dante is not here confusing his arrangement because he distinguishes between the activity of the *predone* who takes another's property by *force*—where force is the essential element—and that of a thief who achieves the same end by *fraudulence*. These latter are dealt with in Ctos. XXIV-XXV where they are not called *predone* but *il ladro* (see Cto. XXIV,38; XXV,1) and their crime, "theft" (*furto*, Cto. XXV,29).

58 On these characters and their crimes see the notes in Sayers' edition of *The Divine Comedy* (Harmondsworth, Penguin, 1949), or those of Singleton in his edition. The true nature of the crime of fraudulent theft is exhibited in the horrifying punishment Dante accords to those who stole on earth. They undergo a continual transformation into vile serpent and lizard forms that are not their own and then back again (Cto. XXV,46f.). The distinction between what is theirs (their own form) and another's is as hopelessly confused in this transmutation as the confusion between "mine" and "thine" which they caused by their fraudulent thievery on earth.

59 For details about the background to this reference to Cacus, see Singleton's commentary on the "Inferno," pp. 431-35. The reader should bear it in mind that Dante will place some murderers even lower than the thieves, as for example Friar Albergio (Cto. XXXIII), but this is because their essential crime is regarded as a form of fraud (in Albergio's case because of his treachery to his brother, Manfred).

60 Translation, Fitzgerald.

61 This position has a long tradition behind it, going back, in the Christian West, at least to the time of Augustine. See, for example, in the *Confessions* where, speaking of the divine justification for corporeal and capital punishment, he says, "your law, O God, permits [human licence] to be stemmed by force. From the schoolmaster's cane to the ordeals of martyrdom, your law prescribes bitter medicine to retrieve us from the noxious pleasures which cause us to desert you" (Pine-Coffin trans., I,xiv,23). It is clear that in finding divine sanction for corporeal and capital punishment, Augustine means that such means are *permitted* by God because they are necessary if the state is to keep peace and order amongst fallen, wicked humanity. See also *City of God* XIX, 14-17. In More's day, Luther was to hold a similar position on the divine sanction of capital force necessary to the government of an unredeemed world. This is explained most clearly in the treatise of 1523, *Secular Authority: To What Extent It Should Be Obeyed*, and is summed up in his famous aphorism from part two of the text: "Frogs need storks."

62 The example of the Polylerites—which Raphael recommends—who countenance capital punishment in certain cases (see 77/35, 79/1, 79/5) shows that he is not opposed to it in principle and without qualification. Nowhere for example does he assert that death is not a just punishment for murder nor, as with the Polylerites, that it should not be the remedy of last resort. This however need not be taken as contradicting his objections on the ground that, at least amongst Christians, Scripture forbids man to kill. As the Yale ed. notes (p. 342, 72/30), "Hythlodaeus' position seems to be that capital punishment is just only for crimes specified by God." I add that it not only *seems* to be so but it *is* so—i.e., this is the way Raphael (and More) reconcile the Scriptural injunction not to kill with the other cases in Scripture where God does allow capital punishment. The absolute principle is "thou shall not kill" and it is permitted for the state to kill, in order to control men's wickedness, only in those cases where there is a specific injunction to do so. Plato also (*Republic* 410a), teaches that "those who are evil-natured and incurable in soul they [the guardians] will themselves put to death."

63 See the references for this position in the Yale ed., p. 342, 72/16 (More/Plutarch), and p. 342, 74/15 (Patrizi/Erasmus).

64 See the notes in the Yale ed. (p. 342, 74/15) for evidence that the Romans were so regarded by the Renaissance Humanists.

65 See especially *Republic* VI (504c)-VII (516e) on the images of the sun, the line and the cave. At 529b,c Socrates says, "I, for my part, am unable to suppose that any other study turns the soul's gaze upward than that which deals with being and the invisible. But if anyone tries to learn about the things of sense, whether gaping up or blinking down, I would never say that he really learns—for nothing of the kind admits of true knowledge—nor would I say that his soul looks up, but down, even though he study floating on his back on sea or land."

66 Though it may seen incredible that any would have been taken in by More's fiction at these points, see the evidence to the contrary at the end of Rhenanus' letter to Pirckheimer (253/20f.), and More's own distinction between the capabilities of the ordinary reader (*vulgi*, 250/4) and the more learned (*litteratioribus*, 250/10), in his second letter to Giles.

67 On the meaning of the name, Polylerites, see the note in the Yale ed. (p. 343, 74/21), where it is translated as the "People of Much Nonsense."

68 Plato makes the point again at 501e where he says, "until the philosophical class wins control, there will be no surcease of trouble for city or citizens nor will the polity which we fable in words be brought to pass in deed." See also Socrates' argument about "the inevitableness of the degeneracy of the majority" (489d,e), which concludes correctly, according to Plato's principles, that "Philosophy, then, the love of wisdom, is impossible for the multitude" (494a). At the end of Book VII Plato

considers what a philosopher would have to do in order to realize the true republic, supposing that such a person ever came to political power in an existing—i.e., corrupt—state. He says that he would have to send out all the inhabitants above the age of ten to work the fields and take over the education of the children to "bring them up in [his] own customs and laws which will be such as we have described" (541a). In other words a philosopher can only rule in a state which is "adapted to his nature" (497a) and this cannot be unless its members have been brought up and formed in the customs and laws dictated by philosophy. It is surely with wry humour that Socrates says, "This is the speediest and easiest way in which a city and constitution as we have portrayed could be established and prosper" (541a). Logically he is correct, but practically he knows very well that it would be the hardest thing in the world to get all the adults to abandon their political interests and concern themselves solely with production (field work) until a right-thinking generation can be produced. To suppose that he intended this as a practical programme for implementing the true state seems to me to ignore its irony and to impose a literal interpretation which is grossly un-Platonic. On this point see also below, n. 69.

69   My interpretation of the strictly theoretical nature of Plato's argument, following on More's own understanding, runs directly counter to a strong tendency in twentieth-century comment which sees Plato's discussion in the opposite sense as having only a practical import and as if he intended it as a blueprint for the construction of an actual "Utopian" state. One of the starkest expressions of this reading, which is also highly antagonistic to Plato, is found in Karl R. Popper, *The Open Society and Its Enemies* (2 vols., 5th ed. rev., Princeton, Princeton University Press, 1966: see especially Vol. 1, *The Spell of Plato*). The literal interpretation has been ably refuted by, among others, V. Goldschmidt (in *Platonisme et pensée contemporaine*, Paris, Aubier, éditions Montagne, 1970, pp. 165-73), but it continues to be maintained as, for example, in the recent work by Cosimo Quarta, *L'Utopia platonica, il projetto politico di un grande filosofo* (Milano, Italia, F. Angeli, 1985).

So much is the practical point of view congenial to modern thought that even an early classic (1926), like that of A. E. Taylor (*Plato, the Man and His Work*, 7th ed., London, Methuen, University Paperback, 1966), cannot avoid it. He maintains that "the political problem of the right organization of a state is avowedly introduced not on its own account, but because we see human virtue and vice 'writ large.' . . . Hence we shall probably be misunderstanding if we imagine, as has sometimes been imagined, that either Socrates or Plato is seriously proposing a detailed new constitution for Athens" (p. 273). Yet we nevertheless find Taylor going on directly to treat of what Socrates says about the first, Arcadian, city not as a strictly theoretical exercise but as related to "what Athens itself had been before the period of victory and expansion which made her an imperial city and the centre of a world-wide sea-borne commerce" (p. 273). In other words, in spite of himself, he interprets the work in relation to particular historical developments. He goes on to say, "In the description of the steps by which this little society expands and becomes a city with a multitude of artificial wants, and trades which minister to them, thus acquiring a 'superfluous population' which must somehow be provided for, we can hardly see anything but a conscious reflection of the actual expansion of Athens under Cimon and Pericles" (p. 274).

But is this how Socrates argues? Is he speaking about real cities, such as Athens, where this development no doubt took place? Socrates does not maintain that his Arcadian state ever existed nor that it *developed* into the luxurious city. Rather, he sees these as two separate theoretical possibilities (a city simply, and a luxurious city, see 372e). It is not as if *Arcadia* acquired a superfluous population that had somehow to be provided for since, in theory, this will not happen where the people do not go "begetting offspring beyond their means" (372c). And likewise it is not some *city* that has enlarged itself but *Socrates and his listeners* who must "enlarge the city again . . .

and swell out its bulk" (373b)—i.e., in theory, in order to have before them a model which is adequate to the very different state of affairs about which Glaucon wants to speak and where the ends of reason are not limited by natural necessity. The argument about whether the *Republic* is to be taken primarily in a practical or in a theoretical sense, and about whether it is really about politics or the soul will, no doubt, rage on and cannot be settled here if it can be settled at all. But this is really incidental to my purpose, as here I only want to maintain that *More* understood Plato's argument as purely theoretical.

70 Descartes expresses this new direction in philosophy—where metaphysics is not the end, as with Aristotle, but the beginning—and whose ultimate fruit is not the knowledge of God but the practical transformation and amelioration of the world, in the image of the tree of philosophy. He says, "Thus philosophy as a whole is like a tree whose roots are metaphysics, whose trunk is physics, and whose branches, which issue from the trunk, are all the other sciences. . . . but just as it is not from the roots or the trunk of the trees that one culls the fruit, but only from the extremities of their branches, so the main use of philosophy [its practical fruit] is dependent on those of its parts that we cannot learn until the end" (*Philosophical Works*, trans. E. S. Haldane and G. R. T. Ross, Cambridge, Cambridge University Press, 1973, Vol. 1, p. 211). Both Machiavelli and Hobbes, who are generally regarded as the foun- tainheads of modern political philosophy (see, for example, Leo Strauss, *Studies in Platonic Political Philosophy*, Chicago, University of Chicago Press, 1983, pp. 211- 12), make the same comment on the relation of their work to all earlier political thought: namely, that theirs is real (i.e., practical) while that of all their predecessors back to Plato was a dream (i.e., mere theory). See Machiavelli, in the famous passage from *The Prince*, 15, and in the Preface to Book I of the *Discourses* where he likens himself to one who "sets off in search of new seas and unknown lands" and who has "decided to enter upon a new way, as yet untrodden by anyone else" (*The Dis- courses of Niccolò Machiavelli*, trans. Leslie J. Walker, London, Routledge & Kegan Paul, 1953). Hobbes too, in the *Leviathan*, was reduced to "the point of believing this my labour, *as useless, as the commonwealth of Plato*" (emphasis mine), but he manages to get over this by the end of the paragraph in the hope that some sovereign will read his ("short, and I think clear") work and will "convert this truth of speculation, into the utility of practice" (ch. 31, p. 241, in the edition of M. Oakeshott, Blackwell's Political Texts, Oxford, Basil Blackwell, n.d.). See also *ibid.*, ch. 46, p. 438, and the *Elements of Law*, ed. Tonnies, Cambridge, 1928, Dedicatory Letter, I,1, sect. 1; 13, sect. 3; 17, sect. 1.

71 On the equation of "scholastic" with "academic" (which latter relates ultimately to the Platonic Academy), see Yale ed., p. 371, 98/6; p. 372, 98/11. There is no reason to suppose that More may not have used the term *philosophia scholastica* as well in deprecation of the "ideas, universalities, separated forms, first matters, quiddities, haecceities, formalities and the like stuff" of late medieval scholastic philosophy— made such fun of, in these words, by Erasmus in his *In Praise of Folly* (trans. J. Wilson, 1668; repr., Ann Arbor, University of Michigan Press, Ann Arbor Paper- backs, 1958, p. 92).

72 See the Yale ed., p. 375, 100/9, for other contemporary references (to Erasmus and Lupset) on the impossibility of realizing the Platonic commonwealth given the cor- rupt nature of actual men and women.

73 The top stage in Plato's image of the line is the point at which thought moves from images, assumptions and hypotheses to the only absolutely scientific (i.e., unhypothetical) knowledge which consists in the knowledge of the Good. See *Repub- lic*, 511b,c, where he writes, "Understand then, said I, that by the other section of the intelligible I mean that which reason itself lays hold of by the power of dialectic, treating its assumptions not as absolute beginnings but literally as hypotheses, under-

pinnings, footings, and springboards so to speak, *to enable it to rise to that which requires no assumption* and is the starting-point of all, and after attaining to that again taking hold of the first dependencies from it, so to proceed downward to the conclusion, making no use whatsoever of any object of sense but only of pure ideas moving on through ideas to ideas and ending up with ideas'' (emphasis mine). See also 510b, ''there is another section [of the intelligible section of the 'line'] in which it [thought] advances from its assumption to a beginning or principle that transcends assumption, and in which it makes no use of the images employed by the other section, relying on ideas only and progressing systematically through ideas.''

On the vexed question of whether God and the Idea of the Good are one and the same to Plato see W. D. Ross, *Plato's Theory of Ideas*, Oxford, Clarendon Press, 1951, pp. 43-45. I think that the best answer is still that of A. E. Taylor (*Plato*, pp. 288-89), who says, ''If the question means 'is the Form of Good another name for *the God recognized in the Platonic* philosophy?' the answer must be definitely, No.... But if we mean 'is the Good spoken of in the *Republic* identical with what Christian divines and philosophers have meant by God?' the answer must be modified.... Thus, as it seems to me, metaphysically the Form of Good is what Christian philosophy has meant by God, and nothing else.''

74 The whole passage runs from 101/19-36.

75 The connection between More, Erasmus and the *devotio moderna* of the Brethren of the Common Life (in which Erasmus was raised and which was very attractive to the Renaissance Humanists) is clearly present in this speech of Raphael's. He, and More, and Erasmus, all assume that the role of the Christian is the *Imitation of Christ*, along the lines laid down by Thomas à Kempis in his work of this title (trans. Richard Whitford, ed. Harold C. Gardiner, 1530; repr., Garden City, N.Y., Image Books, 1955). For a discussion of the lifelong effects of the *devotio moderna* on Erasmus, see J. Huizinga, *Erasmus and the Age of Reformation*, trans. F. Hopman, 1924; repr., New York, Harper & Row, 1957, esp. ch. 1.

76 The text of this famous test of Catholicity comes from Vincent of Lerins' *Commonitorium* (II,3). It reads, ''*quod ubique, quod semper, quod ab omnibus creditum est.*'' Perhaps the simplest and most complete statement of the principles of orthodox exegesis is found in Augustine's *On Christian Doctrine*.

77 On this general point see my ''Augustinian Biblical Exegesis and the Origins of Modern Science,'' forthcoming in *Collectanea Augustiniana*.

78 More has very correctly translated Plato's γράφω (472d,5) = ''to scratch, to draw lines, sketch, draw, paint,'' by the Latin term *delineo* (20/6) = ''to sketch out, delineate.'' Plato uses this image of a painting or drawing repeatedly: 501a-c, 583b, 596e, 597d, 598a, 602d, 603b, 605a, in addition to the references at 472d and following. More's favourite, Augustine, clearly understood Plato's work in this sense: see the text from the *City of God* (II,14) quoted above, Introduction, n. 38.

79 More's sixteenth-century commentators, aware of the difference between the purpose of Plato's image and More's, continually liken the *Utopia* to a painting remarkable for its practical applicability in the real world. See for example *depictam* (20/20) in Giles' letter to Busleyden, or *velut in speculo* (26/28), and *cuius pencillo nobis tam scite depicta est* (28/5) in Desmarais to Giles. On the early commentators' lively sense of the practical intention of More's work, see P. R. Allen, ''*Utopia* and European Humanism,'' pp. 103-104.

80 More skilfully introduces the mention of Utopia in the context of the morning's discussion in a way that heightens our interest by leading the reader through the same process of discovery he and Giles went through with Raphael. At 55/5 he told us that he would relate ''the talk which drew and led him [Raphael] on to mention that commonwealth,'' but then we hear nothing about it for almost twenty pages until, at 89/34, we come to the first time that Raphael alludes to the island. Here it is simply

given in passing as a geographical reference to the land of the Achorians. At the time this could have meant nothing to More and Giles who had never before heard of the place and, because they did not stop Raphael, the reader concludes that at the time they must have regarded it as an insignificant detail. The same thing occurs the second time Raphael mentions Utopia at 97/16-17, again in passing and as a geographical reference. But now, by the repetition, it begins to appear as a point of some importance to Raphael. On the third occasion, soon after, Raphael at last comes out and explicitly equates this state with Plato's republic in the words quoted above in the text.

81 One of the most influential schools of political philosophy in North America today is that of Leo Strauss. Unlike Karl Popper (*The Open Society and Its Enemies*)—who, taking the discussion of the *Republic* as a practical programme, found in Plato the origin of all the evils of totalitarianism, whether of the left or right, which he sees everywhere but in liberal democracy—Strauss and his followers take the opposite tack and look back to Plato with trust and affection as the surest defence against tyranny. Strauss is highly critical and suspicious of the modern freedom that Machiavelli was the first to enunciate—that is to say, of freedom understood without reference to an essential human nature or to transcendent ideals (see, for example, the essay on Machiavelli in *Studies in Platonic Political Philosophy*). Since I claim that More was doing much the same thing I suspect that Straussians will find his doctrines as depressing and destructive as those of his Italian contemporary.

It is certainly no part of my intention in this book to attempt to explain the subtle and important arguments of Strauss, yet it may be as well to state briefly how I see his position. I think that there is much that is true in his criticism of the contemporary enthusiasm for liberal progressive democracy and much that can truly be laid at the door of Machiavelli (or More). Yet his attempt to restore classical political science, with its basis in a normative morality and piety, seems to falter when he becomes silent on the crucial question of what authority, if any, has survived Machiavelli— and which the unphilosophical multitude could reasonably be expected to adopt. In this I agree with the criticism of my colleague George Grant in his fine consideration of the Strauss/Kojève controversy (*Technology and Empire*, Toronto, House of Anansi, 1969—see the chapter on "Tyranny and Wisdom," pp. 81-109). With respect to the Straussian analysis of the modern world, the problem I see is not so much that he has gone too far in claiming that Machiavelli destroyed and perverted everything, but that he has not gone far enough for, in removing God from the political realm, has not Machiavelli also removed the very basis of the public morality which Strauss wants to resurrect? On the other hand, with respect to the ancients, while Strauss certainly does not fail, like Popper, to see the theoretical import of Plato's political teachings, and praises him on that account, it is not at all clear that he is willing to accept the consequences which this entailed for the ancients—i.e., that he would recommend that we should follow Socrates to an unjust death at the hands of an unjust state which, in the modern context, would presumably mean something like a Socratic acceptance of the holocaust, because justice in the individual soul is the only goal that lies within our power to achieve.

82 R. P. Adams, *The Better Part of Valor*, p. 125.

83 Raphael's words are described as *dicta prudenter* (84/31). More is very accurate here. It is not the part of the *modern* philosopher to come to a certain knowledge of eternal truths (i.e., *sapientia*, which *was* the aim of ancient philosophy—see above, n. 73). Where the truth is sought in the world and is dependent on experience, absolute certainty is no longer possible and wisdom appears in the form of prudence = the modern science in which knowledge is not an indubitable and unchangeable certainty but only the most likely or probable account—and one which can change if new facts are uncovered or better theories developed.

84 Logan is surely correct in his view that *Utopia* is not to be understood in the genre of the *speculum principis*. All the same his interpretation of what More is doing leaves him unable to say what More's position *is* on the question which he regards as the core of the discussion in Book I—i.e., are *honestas* and *utilitas* able to be united in practice (see *Meaning*, pp. 121-22)? See also above, n. 32, for my criticism of Logan's general approach.

85 The only explicit connection between Raphael and Plato to this point has been Giles' passing remark on the Platonic nature of Raphael's travels (49/37).

86 On Dionysius, see the note in the Yale ed., p. 350, 86/19-20.

87 See the Yale ed., p. 350, 86/29-30, and the following notes to 88/22.

88 "Utopia," from οὐ+τόπος: "not"+"place" = "Noplace, Nowhere": see Yale ed., p. 385, 112/1-2. "Achoria," from ἀ-privative+χῶρος: "without"+"place" = "Without place": see Yale ed., p. 385, 88/25. By such made-up names, More lets his educated readers know from the first that he is turning to an imaginary example (see More's second letter to Giles, 251/9-21).

89 Compare *Republic* 423b, where Socrates, discussing the proper size of a true city, says, "I think, I said, that they should let it grow so long as in its growth it consents to remain a unity, but no further."

90 It makes no difference to my point that Caracalla only extended citizenship to the whole world so that the whole world could pay the taxes of the Roman citizen.

91 The adjectives come from Hegel's brief but incomparable exposition of Rome in *The Philosophy of History*, trans. J. Sibree, 1899; repr., New York: Dover Publications, 1956.

92 *Junius Brutus* (fl. 510 B.C.), founder of the Republic, put to death his own sons and his wife's brothers because he found them plotting to restore the monarchy of Tarquinius Superbus whose son had raped *Lucretia*, who, to vindicate her virtue and prove she in no way consented to the act, killed herself (the story is told in Livy, *Ab Urbe Condita*, in *Livy*, trans. B. O. Foster et al., Loeb Classical Library, 13 vols. plus Index vol., Cambridge, Mass., Harvard University Press, 1919- , I, 57-II, 5). *Marcus Regulus* (d. 250 B.C.), Roman commander in the first Punic war, was captured by the Carthaginians and sent to Rome in a Carthaginian embassy suing for peace. He advised the senate to continue the war, then, spurning the chance to remain in Rome, because he had sworn to return to Carthage if he failed to obtain the result the enemy desired, went back and was horribly tortured to death (Livy, Epitome of *Ab Urbe Condita*, 16: see also Cicero, *De Officiis* I,3; Horace, *Carmina* 3, 5). *Cato the Younger* (of Utica, 95-46 B.C.), unbending defender of Republican liberty and Stoic virtue, committed suicide rather than live without them under Caesar's rule (Sallust, *Bellum Catilinae* 52f.). For a convenient list and brief statement of the lives of these and other Roman heroes, notable still in late antiquity, see Augustine, *City of God* V, 18.

93 See for example Augustine's evidence about the rites of the Heavenly Mother in *City of God* II, 4 and 26. The Christians of course constituted the one great exception the Romans found themselves forced to make to their principle of remaining indifferent to the particular beliefs of their subjects. Tertullian in his *Apology* is the first to give a clear exposition of the matter and Augustine's *City of God* is the last word on the subject by a contemporary.

94 The terms of the "Cassian Treaty" (*foedus Cassianum*) may be found in Livy, *Ab Urbe Condita* II, 33, 4. H. H. Scullard dates the treaty about 495 B.C. and remarks that "it remains a landmark in the early history of Rome" (*A History of the Roman World 753-146 B.C.*, 4th ed., London and New York, Methuen, 1980, p. 93, and see endnotes).

95 Augustine very clearly understood that this was the principle of Rome. He makes this his point of departure in the Preface to the first book of the *City of God*.

96 Translation, Fitzgerald.

97 Yale ed., p. 384, 110/8. See also the small size of the land of the Polylerites, "who do not try to enlarge their territory" (75/34).

98 I say that the idea of a world commonwealth had its beginnings in Plato because once Plato turns to the consideration of the luxurious city there is no limit, in principle, to its expansion other than the external limit of what its neighbours have the strength to stop.

99 The contest between these two is reflected in the setting of the work. The dispute over wool was between the King of England on the one hand and the Prince who was soon to become the Holy Roman Emperor on the other.

100 An image of the "grotesque" splendour that More must have had in mind can be studied in Dürer's drawings of the triumphal car of the emperor Maximilian (1522). Reproductions are found in Willi Kurth's *The Complete Woodcuts of Albrecht Dürer*, New York, Dover Publications, 1963, plates 312-17.

101 See *Republic* 435e, where Plato speaks of the "love of knowledge" as the peculiar possession of the Greeks.

102 Logan (*Meaning*, p. 69) makes this point, drawing on Surtz (Yale ed., p. 362, 90/28) and Russell Ames, *Citizen Thomas More and His Utopia*, Princeton, Princeton University Press, 1949. See also the other notes in the Yale ed., pp. 361-62, 90/23, 24, which give evidence on the widespread nature of these practices.

103 This is Raphael's second mention of Utopia in the same context and to the same end as before: see above, n. 69. On the name of the Macarians (Μάκαρ = "blessed, happy"), see Yale ed., p. 371, 96/12.

104 On the policy of Henry VII, as moved by this thought, see Yale ed., p. 365, 94/4-5.

105 "οἱ περίοικοι were, in Laconia, the free inhabitants of the country-towns, the remains of the original inhabitants, who enjoyed civil but not political privileges, opp. on the one hand to the Spartans, and on the other to the Helots" (Liddell and Scott, *Abridged Greek-English Lexicon*, art., περίοικος).

106 See the note in the Yale ed., p. 369, 94/32, on *custodem* which "is intended to suggest Plato's *guardian*."

107 So too Machiavelli in *The Prince*, for whom the well-being of the prince depends on the well-being of his subjects, and so he must "abstain from the possessions of his subjects and citizens and from their women" (ch. 17, p. 139; see also chs. 19 and 21 *passim*).

108 Leo Strauss points out that one of the main distinctions between classical and modern political science is that for the ancients "The actualization of the best regime depends on chance, on *Fortuna*, that is, on something which is essentially beyond human control. According to Machiavelli, however, *Fortuna* is a woman who as such must be hit and beaten to be kept under [the reference is to *The Prince*, XXV]; *Fortuna* can be vanquished by the right kind of man" (*Studies in Platonic Political Philosophy*, p. 213). Strauss concludes that "Machiavelli's 'realistic' revolt against tradition led to the substitution of patriotism or merely political virtue for human excellence or, more particularly, for moral virtue and the contemplative life. It entailed a deliberate lowering of the ultimate goal" (*Natural Right and History*, Chicago, University of Chicago Press, 1953, p. 178). In a sense this is quite correct and we have seen the same thing in More, for whom Utopia is neither understood as a realization of Plato's theoretical state which, in More's phrase, carried with it the requirement that "all men were good" (101/3), nor yet, like the medieval state, does it aim at a city beyond this world in Heaven. And, as Strauss says of Machiavelli, we have seen that More too insists that those elements of chance—which Plato thought to be beyond human control—can in fact be controlled by human endeavour. Thus, for example, although fortune had not provided Utopos with the best location, he simply ignored what she

had dealt him and made the place ideal by cutting away the fifteen-mile isthmus (113/7-18) to create the island he desired.

It seems to me that the important question here is why Plato thought that there were certain things which were beyond human control, on which the actualization of the best state depended, while Machiavelli and More recognized no such limitations. Strauss, I think, does not really have an answer except to say that they lowered the goal to what lay within human power—but does this not beg the question? For we might ask if there has not been a radical change in the conception of what lies within human power since, to use this example, More proposes a solution—the removal of an isthmus—which certainly lay within Greek technical competence but which Plato, as it were, would not have considered. And, from the other side, we might ask why all of a sudden, with Machiavelli and More, people decided to turn away from a humanly unrealizable ideal which had sustained and informed political thought for two thousand years? The answer I have suggested lies in the implicitly Christian position of the two moderns who were willing to assume, as the ancients were not, that reason and nature were ultimately one so that nature as such had in it nothing which was in principle impenetrable to reason or beyond its control.

109   In *The Prince*, Machiavelli develops the other side of the modern position and the one which was to be more immediately influential. As Europe moved away from the medieval political system it turned first to the rule of absolute monarchs—strong men in the sense Machiavelli advocated, on whose *person* the well-being of the state depended. All the same, Machiavelli's appeal to the prince is not at all in the *speculum principis* genre and, as we may see in the greatest exponent of absolute monarchy, Hobbes (*Leviathan*, 1651), the work of the absolute monarch is not to impose laws brought down from heaven but to rule through the laws of nature. On this fundamental point More, Machiavelli and Hobbes are all in agreement and it is this which marks their thought as fully modern.

110   See Logan, *Meaning*, p. 114.

111   I maintain this against Logan and Hexter. Hexter says it is "impossible to tell" whether More (the author) sides with Raphael or with his character in this dispute (*More's "Utopia,"* p. 132). Logan says that this "dispute [is not] resolved later in *Utopia*: the question is dropped at this point and is never taken up again" (*Meaning*, p. 122). See also Chambers (*More*, p. 236) who shows very clearly that, in the context of the times, "Once he [More] had entered the king's service, he was no longer a free man." In this situation one had, as Raphael says, only two choices: to bend to the king's will or to be broken by it. See also above, n. 40.

112   See Yale ed., p. 381, 104/29, for other instances of the image of a sick commonwealth.

113   It is often said (see, for example, Logan, *Meaning*, pp. 209ff.) that one of the greatest differences between Plato and More is that the former applied his communism only to the guardian class whereas More extended it to all citizens. This, as we have seen, is not strictly true for in Plato's first-best state (whether in the *Republic* or in the *Laws*), all things are common to all. On this point see below, Conclusion, n. 1.

CONCLUSION

Our study has shown that More's intention in the first book was to prepare the reader for the radically new solution to Europe's political problems contained in the detailed account of Utopia. He has done this by showing that the two fundamental conditions of a happy commonwealth in Plato's *Republic* have no practical application of any possible benefit. Indeed the contrary is the case for, where it is assumed that a separation of the classes is desirable and that it is the business of the philosopher to advise a king, there will follow all the evils of contemporary Europe. This is the criticism of what, in the Platonic teaching, More knew to be inapplicable and destructive. But once Platonism is purged of these elements what remains is the Arcadian paradise. More claimed that this, when properly expanded and developed (as in Book II), would prove to be the salvation of Europe as it struggled out of the collapse of a medieval system that could no longer maintain the balanced relation of sacred and secular powers which had defined European society and politics for a thousand years.

In this essay I do not propose to comment on the second book of the *Utopia*. My intention has only been to help readers do this for themselves through an understanding of More's own introduction. What remains to be clarified is how, in the wider context of the political problem of the sixteenth century, More's criticism of Plato led him to the solution offered in the description of Utopia. If we can answer this question it will be no difficult matter to understand what is going on in Book II.

The problem can be stated in this way. Why did More think that it was possible not only to see but to construct and live in that first-best state, when Plato held this to be an impossibility which lay beyond the power

---

Reference notes to the Conclusion appear on pp. 106-108.

of actual men and women? Human nature had not changed in the interval. More is under no illusion that all men have become good. Why then would the same desire for luxury and owning which made the actual realization of the Arcadian paradise impossible for Plato not make it equally impossible for More? The answer to this question lies in Christianity—in those positions and assumptions that had constituted the warp of the fabric of European life for over a millennium. Indeed, it could hardly be otherwise since More was proposing a solution for Christian Europe. That Utopia did in fact conform to the essential demands of a Christian state is clearly testified in the positions of those humanists who contributed the prefatory materials—amongst whom we may take Rhenanus' letter as an example of the opinion of all. He says:

> The *Utopia* contains principles of such a sort as it is not possible to find in Plato, in Aristotle, or even in the *Pandects* of your Justinian. Its lessons are less philosophical, perhaps, than theirs but more Christian. (253/17-20)

But far from answering our question about how More and his contemporaries thought they could realize what Plato himself only dreamed of, the implicit Christianity of the Utopian institutions only complicates the question. For now we have to answer not only how Christian assumptions made it possible to realize what, for Plato, was impossible, but we have to do this without in any way invoking a knowledge of Christ or the Christian religion which the Utopians did not possess!

This apparently intractable contradiction is what lies behind the opposing interpretations of *Utopia*. Because it seems that one cannot maintain both positions, modern scholars, insofar as they have proposed a complete account of the work, have come down on one side or the other. For some, Utopia is a sacred community, the City of God, fully Christian with its roots in the soil of the medieval church and particularly in the monastic movement from Benedict to St. Francis. For others, it is the purely secular City of Man, having its roots in ancient pagan philosophy and standing as the shining example of what man can, and will in the end, achieve by following the dictates of human nature alone. There is evidently much truth on both sides but so long as they are taken as mutually exclusive it appears that we cannot have the whole truth of More's position—or any fully satisfactory interpretation.

The first point in framing an answer is to recognize that More intended Utopia to be a logical and detailed development of the form of the true and healthy human community as this was recognized by ancient philosophy (in Plato's Arcadia) on the one hand *and* as it had been established and authorized by Christ on the other. He makes this point quite explicitly as the last thing Raphael says in summation of his description of Utopia.

> Nor does it occur to me [says Raphael] to doubt that a man's regard for
> his own interests or the authority of Christ our Saviour—who in his
> wisdom could not fail to know what was best and who in his goodness
> would not fail to counsel what He knew to be best—would long ago
> have brought the whole world to adopt the laws of the Utopian
> commonwealth, had not one single monster, the chief and progenitor
> of all plagues, striven against it—I mean, Pride. (243/26-32)

Raphael observes that there are two identical sources from which the
institutions of Utopia can be thought to arise: "[i] a man's regard for his
own interests or [ii] the authority of Christ our Saviour." In other words
Raphael, who is both a philosopher and a Christian, and thus knows both
sides, affirms that, on the question of the nature of the best commonwealth, human nature teaches the same lesson as Christ.

With Plato this meant that the first-best state (Arcadia) was the one in
which there was no private property, and More understood that Christ
both taught and practised the same thing.[1] Thus the Utopians, solely on
the strength of their fidelity to the dictates of human nature, had arrived
at the same position as Christ. The result was that when Raphael told the
Utopians about Christianity,

> you would not believe [he says] how readily disposed they, too, were
> to join it, whether through the rather mysterious inspiration of God or
> because they thought it nearest to that belief which has the widest
> prevalence amongst them. [But, he adds] I think that this factor, too,
> was of no small weight, that they heard that His disciples' common
> way of life had been pleasing to Christ and that it is still in use among
> the truest societies of Christians.[2] (219/5-8)

More clearly believed that on this question the natural man could,
without any knowledge of Christ, arrive at the same conclusion as Christ
taught in the Gospels. This identity between Utopian practice and the
counsels of the Gospels was easily and universally recognized by More's
humanist friends who contributed to the work. Either by their silence
(had it been anything other they would have objected on the grounds that
Utopia could have had no application in Christian Europe), or explicitly,
all recognized that the Utopians, though without any knowledge of
Christ or Christianity (see 217/36 and Desmarais' letter to Giles, 27/
36-29/5) had, in Budé's words, "adapted the customs and the true
wisdom of Christianity for public and private life and . . . have kept this
wisdom uncorrupted even to this day" (11/6-8). The implication in the
last clause is that the social and political practices of contemporary
Christianity were a corruption of the true and original position of the
Gospel. In this More, Budé, and the Renaissance Humanists of their
mind, all share the same ground as Luther in his use of Scripture to
criticize the contemporary church. The difference is that the former
looked to a renewed fidelity to the Gospel in matters of practice where

Luther and the Reformers did so on questions of doctrine. Budé further echoes Raphael's own judgement that the institutions of the Utopians are "holy" (see Raphael's *sanctissima instituta*, 102/28, and Budé's *sancta instituta*, 12/17), and for this reason he renames Utopia *Hagnopolis* (13/9) or the "Holy City."[3] This would bring to the mind of any Christian the idea that Utopia was the Heavenly Jerusalem, the City of God, realized here on earth—the very thing that the still medieval Dante had thought was incapable of being given an adequate institutional form in this world.[4]

Much as More saw an identity between the teaching of Christ and what the Utopians had accomplished by reason, it is clear all the same that there remains a great difference between the institutions of Utopia and ancient Platonism on the one hand and between it and the institutions of medieval Christendom on the other. Taken together these differences are what distinguish More's solution to the best-commonwealth question from the surpassed position of antiquity and the bankrupt position of the Middle Ages, and they account for the appearance in his work of a truly modern social and political philosophy. Broadly speaking we can say that his aim was to overcome the medieval partnership of two separated powers—without falling back into the political solution of antiquity which organized the state solely in terms of an objective and divine law, whether theoretically (with Plato) or practically (with Rome). The practical form of the ancient state, embodied in its supreme shape in the Roman Empire, was long since dead and was of no use or interest to Christians for all the reasons Augustine had first laid out in his *City of God*. Likewise, as More has shown in the first book, the theoretical solution of Plato, while correct theoretically, had no direct application of any practical benefit.

We must consider each side in turn starting with the difference between Utopia and the Christian institutions in More's day. From its earliest times the Christian religion had recognized that Christ had both practised and counselled a communal way of life for his followers. In the first three centuries this was also largely forced upon the young church by the circumstance of its poverty and persecution. This is well attested in the writings of the Apostolic fathers, Minucius Felix and Tertullian. By the fourth century, with Constantine's Edict of Toleration in 313 and the subsequent adoption of Christianity as the established religion of the Roman Empire, the situation changed rapidly. The communal life of the early church inevitably came into increasing conflict with that most Roman of principles—the legal ownership of property—as wealthier citizens converted and as the civic and military affairs of the empire fell into the hands of Christians. Ambrose and Augustine established the fundamental lines on which the Latin West was to solve the problem. The Western Christian empire was to be ruled by a partnership of *two* separate powers, church and state, both deriving ultimately from God, but with distinct spheres of interest and competence.[5] The strict communism of the Gospels was to be embodied in the *religious* life which, after Benedict of Nursia (*c*. 525), was chiefly located in the monasteries that soon spread throughout the length and breadth of Europe as a paradise in the wilderness of this world and an earthly anticipation of the City of God.[6] Alongside this, but separated from it, there existed the *secular* culture which, though thoroughly Christian, was organized along the lines of the virtuous state as conceived by the ancient philosophers. Here private property and marriage were permitted as necessary to the continuance and government of the world. The religious side was essentially pacific, the secular inevitably and justly concerned with war. Although both sides in this partnership were founded on Dominical authority,[7] the religious life in the monasteries was held to be the higher and truer form of Christianity because it was both grounded in the form of life adopted by Christ and because it was concerned primarily with the eternal and spiritual end of man—whereas the secular was concerned with the lower aspects of his temporal and bodily well-being.

More clearly held this opinion, as we see from the approving words he put in Raphael's mouth: "His [Christ's] disciples' common way of life had been pleasing to Christ and . . . it is still in use amongst the *truest (germanissimos) societies of Christians*" (219/6-8, emphasis mine—the clause refers to the monastic way of life[8]). From this point of view it is possible to see Utopia as a gigantic monastery—as if what More had proposed as an answer to the political problem was to apply to the world at large that monastic form of life which had developed as the "truest offshoot" (*germanus* = genuine, real, actual, true; from *germen* = offshoot, bud) of the organization of the human community that had been adopted by Christ himself.

The proponents of this view have noted correctly the many similarities between Utopia and the medieval monasteries.[9] In both there were no private possessions and a complete inward-looking self-sufficiency was the aim of the community. In both, the most minute details of daily life were lived under a rigid rule (see the *regula CHRISTI* that Raphael praises at 100/25-26) which ordered the proper mixture of manual work and study; where dress, sexual activity and movement from place to place were controlled; where families were rotated from house to house as monks from cell to cell; where meals were communal with moral instruction; where the day was divided in a way reminiscent of the canonical hours; where there was regular prayer and confession; where there was a love of gardens; and where the officials—like the abbot of a monastery or the prioress of a convent—were elected. These points of similarity, and others, can easily be verified by comparing the account of Utopia with the various monastic rules from Augustine to that of the Carthusians.

All this is true, yet what we must attend to are the differences between Utopia and the monastery since it is in these respects that More was able to move beyond the collapsing division of the sacred and secular that was the root cause of the problem in his day. Here the chief and only point to note is that this monastic way of life amongst the Utopians, if this is what it is to be called, was in no way separated from a secular society operating independently and alongside it as in the Middle Ages. What More took to be the essence of Christ's teaching about the true and healthy form of the human community was the communal way of life. Throughout the Middle Ages this had been embodied in the monastic movement and it was *this* aspect of the latter that he now proposed should be made the rule for a secular state. But in order to do this he had to cut off from monasticism everything which was exclusively religious (i.e., the monastic vows of poverty, chastity and obedience) and everything which assumed a secular partner (the Christian state), to look after those inescapable matters with which a "religious" could not concern himself (i.e., the policing and punishment of criminals, and matters of war).

These things are just what distinguish Utopia from the monastery. Utopians, unlike monks or nuns, do not have to take vows to become members of the community. They are such by the natural right of birth. They do not have to adopt a position of ascetic poverty, but rather the state aims at "all that is requisite for either the necessity *or the convenience* of living" (129/34-35, emphasis mine) and both of these are equated with "pleasure as their end and happiness" (167/6). And by this they understand "every movement and state of body or mind in which, under the guidance of nature, man delights to dwell" (167/7-9).[10] Thinking "that no kind of pleasure is forbidden, provided no harm comes of it" (145/24-26), they enjoy "excellent and sumptuous meals" (141/30) with pleasant music, delicacies for desert, burnt spices and perfumes (145/20-23), the pleasures of sex (173/23) and bodily attractions (189/19) and, on the whole, are characterized by Raphael as "easy-going, good-tempered, ingenious and leisure-loving" (179/38-39). Unlike the religious and monastic chastity, the Utopians marry after mutual naked inspection, have sexual relations and children (187/27-189/25), and none are bound by any special vows of obedience, being free to choose their craft (127/15-22), place of work (187/13-20), mates (187/39), whether or not to fight in foreign wars (209/26) and their religion (221/3-4 and 27-28). And obviously, unlike the monastery, the Utopian state both punished crimes and waged war.

All of this would certainly have been seen as totally incompatible with a truly religious or holy community from the standpoint of the medieval period. The whole of Europe had been crying out for reform amongst priests, monks and friars because they more and more did just these secular things.[11] But More saw that the answer could not lie in urging them back to their true calling by pious platitudes and moral suasion. This was as futile an endeavour as it was to imagine that philosophers, by their exhortations to virtuous behaviour, could move secular rulers to good ends. Even if this could have worked it would only have pushed the world back into the Middle Ages with nothing to prevent the same thing happening all over again. A more radical solution was required. More provides it by asserting that any Christian who looks to the Gospel rather than to the practices which, over the centuries, had developed and solidified in the Church, must concede that, *just insofar as the question of the best commonwealth was concerned*, all that Christ had actually taught was a common way of life and what could reasonably be deduced from this principle. All the rest in the medieval version of the best and truest community (i.e., the monastery)—its vows of poverty, chastity and obedience, the disinterest in nature, its asceticism and mortifications—were secondary and inessential to the really holy form of human society as practised and counselled by Christ and as embodied in the Utopians who think that

> to despise the beauty of form, to impair the strength of the body, to turn nimbleness into sluggishness, to exhaust the body by fasts, to injure one's health, and to reject all the other favours of nature, unless a man neglects these advantages to himself in providing more zealously for the pleasure of other persons or of the public, in return for which sacrifice he expects a greater pleasure from God—but otherwise to deal harshly with oneself for a vain and shadowy reputation of virtue to no man's profit or for preparing oneself more easily to bear adversities which may never come—this attitude they think is extreme madness and the sign of a mind which is both cruel to itself and ungrateful to nature, to whom it disdains to be indebted and therefore renounces all her benefits. (177/38-179/11)

The Utopians (and More) *do* allow a secondary place in the state for the expression of these secondary desires. They are not essential to the nature of the best commonwealth as such and consequently they are understood to be strictly voluntary and are explicitly adopted for religious motives alone. Of course just these two things distinguished the "religious" life in the medieval system but the difference is that there it existed *alongside* the state whereas in Utopia it exists *within* it; i.e., not as a competing version of the true human community but as the expression of purely individual piety in persons who "for religious motives eschew learning and scientific pursuit and yet allow themselves no leisure" (225/27-29).[12] This is the modern position where matters of belief are not taken as the basis of public institutions (i.e., the *res publica*, in its literal sense of the "public business"), but as the private and voluntary concern of individuals. In Utopia these religious types voluntarily do all the hard, rough and filthy work, to "secure leisure for the others and yet *claim no credit for it*" (226/39-227/1, emphasis mine). That is, they do not insist, like the degenerate monks, friars and clergy of More's day, that what they do for *private* and religious reasons is or ought to be the basis and model of the *public* good. Seeking their reward from God's grace, in heaven, the "religious" in Utopia do not demand, as a right, any reward from the state for what they have voluntarily undertaken. This is just the opposite of the "severe and sour" (*torvitatem*, 82/16) friar at Morton's whose anger sprang from the suggestion that the state should not recognize and credit the sacrifices of his mendicant life—and treat him as, what he was from the point of view of the state, a beggar amongst beggars. Very different are the holy men in Utopia.

> Of these persons there are two schools. The one is composed of celibates who not only eschew all sexual activity but also abstain from eating flesh meat and in some cases from eating all animal food. They entirely reject the pleasures of this life as harmful. They long only for the future life by means of their watching and sweat. Hoping to obtain it very soon, they are cheerful and active in the meanwhile.
>
> The other school is just as fond of hard labor but regards matrimony as preferable.... They avoid no pleasure unless it interferes with their labor. They like flesh meat just because they think that this fare makes them stronger for any work whatsoever. The Utopians regard these men as the saner but the first-named as the holier [they are called "Buthrescae" or "religious par excellence," 227/23-25]. If the latter based upon argument from reason their preference of celibacy to matrimony and of a hard life to a comfortable one they would laugh them to scorn. Now, however, since they say they are prompted by religion, they look up to and reverence them. (227/4-21)

The point is clear: celibacy, the abstention from pleasure, turning away from the investigation of nature and unremitting hard work—all of which were taken as the essential characteristics of the holy *community* in the medieval version—are now restricted to an *individual* piety just because they are voluntary. As such, the Utopians claim they can only be justified on religious grounds coming from the belief in a divine revelation. And their view of God, like the view of Plato who taught that "for the divine... all rules fail" (492e), acknowledges that it lies in God's power to reveal himself when, how and to whom he wills (see 179/13-15). But the Utopians also know that belief cannot be forced. They are convinced "that it is in no man's power to believe what he chooses" (223/7-8), and so they insist that each person be left "free to choose what he believes" (221/2-223/15). Because what may be demanded by a man's private belief goes beyond what is demanded of all men in virtue of their reason, it cannot be used as the basis for a universal community—unless, of course, all men share the same belief—which, in fact they do not, either in Utopia or Europe.[13] In bringing religion "within" the state in this way—i.e., by removing it as a separated power which proposes a competing version of the true community— More had arrived at the truly modern position.

———————————

This criticism of the mistaken notions of contemporary Christianity which had confused revelation with reason is only one side of More's attack on the current hopeless situation of Europe. He is equally critical and equally radical in his attack on the secular side of the medieval equation. The original medieval position had understood that, in the partnership between church and state, the state was to be constructed, not on the basis of revelation but on purely natural grounds as determined by reason. From its start in the Roman Empire, medieval Christendom had borrowed its idea of the state from those ancient philosophers who had considered the question most thoroughly—amongst whom for More and his humanist friends Plato was the foremost spokesman.

In his own day More saw that the secular states of Europe, whether he looked to the dying Holy Roman Empire or to the newly emerging nation states, were organized along Platonic principles—i.e., that all attempted to embody in some sort the separation of the classes and the rule of a philosopher-king which led them to be concerned above all else with war and glory. Just as he insists that the Church had confused revelation with reason in the question of the best commonwealth, so here on the secular side he insists that all the states of Europe have similarly confused the theoretical with the practical. They had done this by attempting to bring an ideal or theoretical city down from the heavens to impose it on this world. They had taken the Platonic prescriptions which were developed solely to assist thought in the discovery of the intelligible nature of justice, confused them with the actual practice of real states and attempted to make them the direct principle for ordering every moment of daily life—as for example in hanging every thief. This confusion does not occur anywhere in antiquity nor in Plato himself, who recognizes that in actual practice men only have it in their power to achieve the second-best constitution because the theoretical and practical, the ideal and the sensible, however much the latter may be made to *resemble* the former, are not and cannot be made identical in all things by any human agency.

But in the medieval world the identity of these two sides was at the very basis of Christian belief. Christ was the eternal Word of God fully incarnate or embodied in the sensible. Consequently, when, according to the medieval formula, a secular state was envisaged alongside the Church and in partnership with it, it was inevitable that it would eventually come to see itself as the earthly form and extension of the heavenly city. By More's day all the European states were maintaining just this—with the disastrous consequences Raphael describes in both books of *Utopia*.[14] And no one would do it more vigorously than More's own king, Henry VIII, in his coming breach with the pope.

Supposing that it lay in man's power to embody the intelligible truth literally and directly—because this is what had been accomplished in Christ—they had taken the two fundamental features of Plato's account of the ideal city and attempted to make them the basis of the secular state. To do this, More has shown, is like taking the ideal circle from the heavens—perfect, adamantine and immutable—hammering it over some wooden wheel on earth and then, while inevitably smashing some parts of the latter in the process, claiming that the truth had been embodied and congratulating oneself on the accomplishment.

Unlike Europeans, the Utopians do not make this confusion and are not so foolish as to attempt to embody, in practice, an ideal of justice which is, according to the hypothesis, theoretical. They are saved from this confusion simply because they have not been corrupted by Christianity. The problem, says More to his contemporaries, is that because you believe that, in Christ, God has united man to himself, you now suppose yourselves, as men, placed in God's position and called to his work—i.e., as rulers, to embody "from above" the ideal, eternal intelligible truth and, as ruled, to conform "from below" to a divine truth. But this assumption is false and a perversion of the true Christian position. The perfect union of heaven and earth, which Christians *do* believe Christ to be, lies in the power of God alone. In insisting on this More is only echoing the constant position of orthodoxy down through the centuries.

If the direct embodiment of the ideal or theoretical city in a worldly state was not the proper goal of corrupt man—points on which both Plato, More and the Church agreed—what was? More's answer is Utopia—which he took to be the teaching of the *Republic* shorn of its theoretical aspects. This amounted to the rational expansion and development of that first Arcadian city—the "true and healthy state" or, in Glaucon's scornful version, the "city of pigs" from which Plato began. A this-worldly, sensible paradise is thus the point of contact between Plato and Christ, between reason and revelation.

The difference between Plato and the Utopians is, however, very great. Plato did not attempt to realize the Arcadian paradise in his concern to discover the theoretical nature of justice and the ideal city. Apart from a sure and certain knowledge of these he believed that men could only flounder in the dark amongst competing and contradictory opinions of the nature of the true state—much like the inconclusive search for justice in Book I of the *Republic*. But, once he had discovered the nature of the ideal city, Plato was forced to conclude that its realization in this world, while theoretically possible granted a lucky set of circumstances and the favour of some god, was beyond the power of the actual men and women from whom his argument had started with Glaucon's request for benches and tables—i.e., those already corrupted by the habit of luxury and the desire for an ownership which establishes each one against all others. Plato can therefore offer the first-best solution only on a theoretical level (in the *Republic*): in practice he was forced to the second-best solution of the *Laws*.

More, not a whit less sober and realistic in his estimate of the habitual corruption of real men and women, nevertheless believed that it was possible not only to see, but to construct and live in that first-best state. The whole difference between More's infectious hope for a brave new world and Plato's philosophical resignation to settle for the second-best turns on the difference in what they believed and this has nothing to do with Christianity in any *explicit* sense. More is absolutely clear that the Utopians established their perfect city without any knowledge of Christ: he supposed it to be the form of the true human community which can be created by consulting reason alone.

More and Plato both agree on the starting point (corrupt man) and the end (Utopia/Arcadia): the whole difference between them is solely about the means or way of getting from the one to the other. Plato assumes that the only road lies through the *mediation of the theoretical*—that the unlimited reason which is the cause of men's falling out of Arcadia can only be restored to order and health by finding its limit in the stable, intelligible divine truth which is its ground. The Utopians on the other hand, with that *implicit* Christian faith which is open to all men at all times and is every bit as justified as its opposite, hold that by divine agency the sensible and the intelligible are one. Nothing man *knows* can prove the contrary and although men cannot know *how* this is so, since this belongs to the inscrutable things of God, they can *believe* it. This belief is at the basis of the whole Utopian commonwealth. Thus, while Utopos "made the whole matter of religion an open question and left each one free to choose what he should believe" (221/27-28), nevertheless, at the same time,

> By way of exception, he conscientiously and strictly gave injunction that no one should fall so far below the dignity of human nature as to believe that souls likewise perish with the body or that the world is the mere sport of chance and not governed by any divine providence. (221/28-32; see also 217/18-26 and 161/30-163/5)

We earlier spoke of the Utopian toleration of all beliefs. This position may seem like a contradiction and the more so when we recall that Raphael goes on to tell how the Utopians "do not regard [a man of this mind] even as a member of mankind . . . so far are they from classing him among their citizens whose laws and customs he would treat as worthless if it were not for fear" (221/35-39). As a consequence, while the Utopians "do not punish him in any way" (223/7), they nevertheless take from him all civil rights, tender him no honour, entrust him with no office, put him in charge of no function, and forbid him to speak his views publicly (see 223/4-15). This does not look like religious toleration—but the reason Utopos made this "exception" is that these beliefs are not on a par with other religious beliefs. These two *can* be established by reason whereas the others *cannot*. In other words More recognized that while most may hold them (or not) in the form of belief, they can be shown by reason as well. As Raphael says, "Though these principles belong to religion, yet they hold that reason leads men to believe and to admit them" (163/3-5).[15]

More could say that these two things can be established by reason because he knew that Plato and the ancient philosophers after him had come to a knowledge of both through philosophy. The difference between the ancients and the Utopians is that the former, knowing they did not know *how* providence worked, were unwilling to construct a state in this world on the supposition that every detail of daily life in this world was governed by divine providence. The ordering of things in this world they chose to believe was man's affair alone and this is exactly the charge that Augustine levels against the Romans at the beginning of the *City of God*.[16]

The Utopian state, on the contrary, is founded on the belief that, by divine institution, the natural and rational are one, both in heaven (which the ancient philosophers knew), *and* here on earth (which the ancients refused to believe). Consequently they have sought to find a cure and limit of man's disordered reason which will work in this world, not indirectly through the intelligible realm, but directly through the *mediation of nature*. Thus,

> The Utopians define virtue as living according to nature *since to this end we were created by God*. That individual, they say, is following the guidance of nature who, in desiring one thing and avoiding another, obeys the dictates of reason. (163/22-26, emphasis mine)

It is this *implicit* Christianity that prevents the Utopians from simply falling back into the social and political solutions of antiquity, while at the same time it in no way makes their solution dependent on any special revelation or a belief that is the possession of some but not all. This is exactly what Beatus Rhenanus meant when he says in his letter to Willibald Pirckheimer, councillor to the Emperor Maximilian, that

> The *Utopia* contains principles of such a sort as it is not possible to find in Plato, in Aristotle, or even in the *Pandects* of your Justinian [i.e., in the political texts of major importance for both Antiquity and the Middle Ages]. Its lessons are less philosophical, perhaps, than theirs, but more Christian. (253/17-20)

There is one final point. Because the Utopians assume that the rational order is contained and discovered in the natural world it follows that none of their solutions can be thought to have the absolute stability of truths derived from the eternal, unchanging intelligible realm. As a result, while Raphael opines that "They have adopted such institutions of life as have laid the foundations of the commonwealth not only most happily, but also to last forever, as far as human prescience can forecast" (245/7-9), yet it nevertheless remains a permanent possibility that these institutions can be improved. The fluidity of both nature and experience opens the door to the possibility of continual progress and improvement—such, for example, as we see in the differences between Plato's Arcadia and More's Utopia. Here too More has come to a properly modern conception of the state. Utopos had recognized this (see 121/26-29) and it was still recognized 1,760 years later (121/30) in the prayer of every Utopian that

> If he errs in these matters or if there is anything better or more approved by God than that commonwealth or that religion, he prays that He will, of His goodness, bring him to the knowledge of it, for he is ready to follow in whatever path it may lead him. But if this form of a commonwealth be the best and his religion the truest, he prays that then He may give him steadfastness and bring all other mortals to the same way of living and the same opinion of God—unless there be something in this variety of religions which delights His inscrutable will. (327/17-26)

The provisional nature of the Utopian's solution—the fact that it allows of improvement—gives us the key to understanding More's final words in the book where he says:

> When Raphael had finished his story, many things came to my mind which seemed very absurdly established in the customs and laws of the people described—not only in their method of waging war, their ceremonies and religion, as well as their other institutions, but most of all in that feature which is the principal foundation of their whole structure. I mean their common life and subsistence—without any exchange of money. This latter alone utterly overthrows all the nobility, magnificence, splendor, and majesty which are, in the estimation of the common people, the true glories and ornaments of the commonwealth. (245/17-26)

This text has given modern interpreters no end of trouble in deciding what More meant by putting these words in the mouth of his character, since they seem to undercut the reader's natural assumption that Utopia *is*, in fact, *More's own* idea of the best commonwealth. This, and the apparently similar thoughts from More's second letter to Giles (see 249ff.), have led some, like J. W. Allen in his *History of Political Thought in the Sixteenth Century*, to see "Book II as only a 'fairy tale' (p. 154) pieced together of ideals that More knew would remain unrealized and whimsical elements 'calculated rather to amuse than to suggest' (p. 154)'' (as stated by Logan, *Meaning*, p. 24).

The sophisticated Logan, on the other hand, while clearly recognizing the irony in the text quoted above, and wanting strongly to see *Utopia* as a serious work of political philosophy, nevertheless finds that in the end More

> dissociates himself from his commonwealth by putting its description into the mouth of Hythloday, by putting disavowals of it in his own mouth, and by peppering the description with mocking names. (*Meaning*, p. 248)

According to Logan, More does this because

> the enormous attractiveness of a sensibly planned society does not lead More either to underestimate the difficulties of realizing one or to downplay the fact that his model is problematic. Neither Hythloday nor the character More imagines that Europe *will* adopt the laws of the Utopian commonwealth, and More's final criticism of Utopia (p. 245) reemphasizes the questionable aspects of this system. (*Meaning*, p. 251)

The great difficulty here is that it leaves us nowhere. If we carefully consider the points which the character More criticizes in this text they are not merely ''questionable aspects,'' but the very whole and substance of Utopia. What is left that is not questionable if one can do away with ''their method of waging war, their ceremonies and religion, as well as their other institutions, but most of all in that feature which is the principal foundation of their whole structure [i.e., their common life and sustenance]''? The answer *must* lie elsewhere unless we are satisfied to accept the conclusion that the work really is a *jeu d'esprit* — a sandcastle which More laboriously constructs in seventy-odd pages only to see it washed away by a single wave at the end.

More provides the solution himself. His *character* is simply reacting with the habitual reflexes of all ordinary readers. He makes this point explicitly when he goes on to say right after these ''criticisms'':

> I knew, however, that he [Raphael] was wearied with his tale, and I was not quite certain that he could brook any opposition to his views, particularly when I recalled his censure of others on account of their fear that they might not appear to be wise enough, unless they found some fault to criticize in other men's discoveries. I therefore praised their way of life and his speech and, taking him by the hand, led him in to supper. I first said, nevertheless, that there would be another chance to think about these matters more deeply and to talk them over with him more fully. If only this were some day possible! (245/27-36)

The last sentence marks the final transition from the character More back to More the author at the time he wrote these last words. Evidently what had seemed "very absurdly established" in every aspect on the first hearing had, with the reflection that only time can bring (see the Utopian regulation on this score, 123/30-125/24), made the institutions of the Utopians appear far less foolish than at first blush. More is gently urging his readers not to condemn the Utopians out of hand, as he had at first been wont to do, but to take time to reflect on the value and virtue of their system.

There remains however a *residue* that not even More the author can accept at the time of writing—months after "he" had heard Raphael. This is clear in the penultimate sentence which expresses his present opinions as the author of the work. "Meanwhile," he says, "though in other respects he [Raphael] is a man of the most undoubted learning as well as of the greatest knowledge of human affairs, I cannot agree with *all* that he said" (245/37-39, emphasis mine). From his standpoint at the time of writing it now seems that the *whole thing* is not to be thrown out but only some parts and, as we may learn from his second letter to Giles, these are not the great and essential matters in its constitution but only "*some little absurdities* [that] exist in the institutions of Utopia . . . *some* things not expedient[ly] enough [devised] in the framing of a commonwealth" (245/29-31, emphasis mine).

What would these be? In part they are those elements in Utopia for which a better or more rational practice can be found. To any of his contemporaries who could come up with such improvements More and the Utopians would certainly say "Thank you"—and adopt them at once. For the most part however More probably had in mind those elements in Utopia which would be contrary to the Christian religion and would therefore present a problem to his audience. The list might (?) include such things as the mutual naked inspection of couples intending to marry (189), Utopian divorce (189-91), married and women priests (229), the projected consecration of a bishop without apostolic succession (219), euthanasia and state-approved suicide (187). More does not say which things he "cannot agree" with but the argument has shown that they cannot be very many or very important because the only modifications he would allow Christians are those which can be justified on the basis of an explicit revelation in the Gospel. And the Utopians themselves would either willingly adopt them as improvements because they were consonant with reason, or else they would tolerate them if, like the lives of the Buthrescae, they could not be grounded in reason but depended on revelation alone. Only in the corrupt nations of Europe would a man like More have to put his head on the chopping-block so that he could be "The king's good servant, but God's servant first."[17] More died as he had lived—the first citizen of Utopia.

More's very last words at the end of the book are these: "I readily admit that there are very many features in the Utopian commonwealth which it is easier for me to wish for in our countries than to have any hope of seeing realized" (245/39-247/3). No doubt More himself did not imagine that England or any other European state would literally adopt the laws of the Utopian commonwealth, abolish private property and turn to a communistic way of life. But our study has shown that he clearly saw the way out of the collapsing social and political system of the medieval period and that he has truly described all the essential characteristics of the modern state in its distinction from the ancient and medieval forms. In the *Utopia* More has pointed out the way in which the modern state was to develop and the ends towards which it is still tending. It would be moronic to ask more of More.

Notes to the Conclusion

1 The classic Scriptural passages are Acts 2:44-45, 4:32-35. By the fact that More does not feel he has to prove the point, we may take it for granted that he understood that all Christians would acknowledge that a communistic way of life was what Christ had both practised and counselled. Budé, for example, has no trouble with the idea and says the same himself (Letter to Lupset, 9/35-11/2). See also the references to Erasmus' similar opinions in the Yale ed., p. 273, 8/25-26; 8/26, and the references to Colet, More and Erasmus, p. 519, 218/5-6.

On the other hand, one might object that it is well known that Plato limits his communism, that is, the community of goods, women and children, to the class of guardians and that it is not extended to the class of craftsmen and farmers who would be the only citizens in Arcadia. Thus it seems that it is not right for me to speak of Arcadia as a state in which there is no private property—and all the more so since some form of private property is presupposed in the exchange of goods which goes on there. I object to this interpretation for two reasons. On the one hand I think it is wrong to read back into Arcadia a class distinction which only appears in Plato in relation to the luxurious city—one might just as well say that all its citizens are kings as craftsmen since the distinction has not yet appeared. My second objection is the one I have already raised (above, Commentary on Book I, n. 52) that, while we must allow some form of private property in Arcadia, it certainly does not and cannot mean the same thing as private property in the luxurious city—i.e., what is held by each against all others. In Arcadia everyone has a share in what everyone else produces and this is not what is meant by private property in the luxurious city. The very concept of ownership—whether private or communal—can only arise where, on the one hand, there is an abstract understanding of property so that I can be thought to "own" something in some other way than by actually consuming or occupying it—and this idea has not yet arisen in Arcadia. And, on the other hand, private property depends on the concept of an individual person with rights against the whole. So far as there is any such "person" in Arcadia it would by the city itself which can either provide, or not, the necessities of nature to its members. The individual members of the Arcadian state have no more an independent identity against the whole than does the liver have "rights" against the rest of our body. Like the Arcadians we either feed all our organs or we feed none. It is in this sense that I speak of Arcadian communism and it is the same thing we find in Utopia—both of which are distinguished from the communism of the Platonic guardians in that in Arcadia, as in Utopia, commonly held property is not set against an independently existing concept of private property.

2 This, "truest societies of Christians," refers to the monastic communities. The ease with which the Utopians adopt improvements coming from the Old World—chiefly, but not only (see 109/1-11, 183/1-185/2), the Christian religion—contrasts sharply with the reluctance of Europeans to adopt the better social and political institutions of the Utopians. This characteristic of the Utopians is stressed over and again from the *Tetrastich* (19/21-27) to Raphael's peroration at the end of Book II (237/37f.)—as is the European pigheadedness which will not change bad ways (see, for example, 57/39-59/17, 109/12-20 and More's wistful words at the end, 247/1-3). The reason for the Utopian pliability and the European rigidity is that the latter think they derive truth in these matters from the stable and unchanging world of the Platonic forms whereas the former find it in the ever-changing face of nature.

3 Giles, too, calls Utopia a "Holy Commonwealth" in his marginal note (147/23).

4 See the discussion about Dante's view of the irreconcilable nature of the *institutions* of church and empire, above, p. 7. In "Paradiso," in the cantos on the first eight heavens, he shows how—under what conditions and in what sense—according to the medieval view, it is possible for the kingdom of God to be realized on earth: as individuals we can be members of the Heavenly City even in this life but that City cannot be identified, simply, with any earthly institution. In this Dante agrees with Augustine's teaching in the *City of God*.

5 The earliest notable conflict between church and state in the West is that between Ambrose and Theodosius. See Ambrose, *Letter LI*.

6 On this general topic see George Hunston Williams, *Wilderness and Paradise in Christian Thought*, New York, Harper, 1962.

7 The great text in this context is the word of Christ, "Render unto Caesar the things that are Caesar's, and to God the things that are God's." It is found in all three of the Synoptic Gospels: Mt. 22:21, Mk. 12:17, Lk. 20:25.

8 More, along with many humanists, had little respect for the mendicant friars. See the story of the friar at Morton's (83/19f.), and the notes in the Yale ed., p. 409, 130/2; p. 536, 226/2.

9 See the texts cited above, Introduction, n. 4.

10 Very different is Augustine's catalogue of the five senses in the *Confessions* X, 30-4. For Augustine the problem is to distinguish which bite of food (or sight, smell, touch or sound) is strictly *necessary*, and thus a good for Christians, and which bite, etc. is over this limit and a temptation to concupiscence which Christians must flee. Augustine's view informed the religious life in Europe from his own time to More's.

11 Huizinga's *Waning of the Middle Ages* provides as good an account as any of the excesses of worldliness (and asceticism) in the religious life of the late medieval period: see esp. chs. 1, 2, 12-17.

12 What distinguishes the "religious" in Utopia from the rest is that they alone are restricted (restrict themselves) *to manual work* while others do manual work with the aim of getting *free from it*—chiefly, but not only (see 129/8-12) for intellectual pursuits (see 129/2, 131/35-133/5). This is the opposite of the monastic model. Throughout the whole of the early Middle Ages the "religious" were, for the most part, the only ones in Europe who could engage in intellectual pursuits. In the later Middle Ages the Dominicans were founded as a religious order devoted exclusively to study and preaching.

13 Most of the early modern political philosophy treats separately of secular and ecclesiastical states. The latter are not organized simply on the basis of the common nature of mankind and presuppose a community of *belief* amongst the citizens: so, for example, Machiavelli in *The Prince* and Hobbes in his *Leviathan*.

14 It is important not to overlook the fact that More's criticism of Europe is not restricted to Book I but continues through the whole of the second book as well.

15 More does not stop to give us the proof for these two points which he says reason can establish on its own. A century later Descartes will take the trouble to do just this and for precisely the same reason—i.e., as the necessary preliminary and basis for the secular government of this world. In his letter to the "Dean and Doctors of the Sacred Faculty of Theology in Paris," to whom his *Meditations on First Philosophy* are dedicated, he writes: "I have always considered that the two questions respecting God and the Soul were the chief of those that ought to be demonstrated by philosophical rather than theological argument. For although it is quite enough for us faithful ones to accept by means of faith the fact that the human soul does not perish with the body, and that God exists, it certainly does not seem possible ever to persuade infidels of any religion, indeed, we may almost say, of any moral virtue, unless, to begin with, we prove these two facts by means of natural reason" (Descartes, *Philosophical Works*, trans. Haldane and Ross, p. 133).

16 Augustine writes: "I know how great is the effort needed to convince the proud of the power and excellence of humility, an excellence which makes it soar above all the summits of this world, which sway in their temporal instability, overtopping them all with an eminence not arrogated by human pride, but granted by divine grace. For the King and Founder of this City which is our subject has revealed in the Scripture of his people this statement of the divine Law, 'God resists the proud, but he gives grace to the humble.' This is God's prerogative; but man's arrogant spirit in its swelling pride has claimed it as its own, and delights to hear this verse [*Aeneid* VI, 853] quoted in its own praise: 'To spare the conquered, and to beat down the proud'" (*City of God*, Book I, preface, trans. Bettenson, p. 5). Augustine took this line from the *Aeneid* as the briefest and most complete statement of how the Romans, at least from the start of the Empire, understood their task and calling in the world. *They* were to bring, or impose, the will of Jupiter (*fatum*) on all mankind, mediating, as it were, between God and world. Augustine objects that in truth only God himself can unite these two sides and that this imperial plan involves a presumptuous arrogance which led the Romans to suppose that, merely because they had correctly recognized the divine principle to which all mankind was subject, it was given to them to play God's role—meting out rewards and punishments—as if they not only knew the abstract truth or law, but could also judge how, in God's eyes, each and every concrete particular in the world stood in relation to that truth. In the first ten books of the *City of God* he points to the two main areas where the folly of this presumption showed itself. On the one hand it is present in their toleration of every sort of perverted and immoral behaviour both in private and public life in both their secular and sacred pursuits. In the Vergilian idiom his complaint here is that Juno's side of things—the realm of chance, accident and the particular, of all that was not held to be governed by "any law of *fatum*" (*Aeneid* XII, 879)—was, falsely, given far too great a scope as things were either permitted or omitted in complete disregard to what, on their own account, *fatum* required of us. On the other hand Augustine shows that the divine law, *fatum*, or Jupiter's side of things, was falsely forced into areas in which it had no concern and here he points chiefly to Rome's intolerance of the Christian religion which could not be justified on its own principles.

17 For details of More's life and death see Stapleton (*Life*) or Roper (*Lyfe*). In Utopia, More would probably have been one of the religious. He tells us that he would have been a monk in England were it not for his duty to his wife and children and Roper reports that "Secretly next to his body, he wore a shirt of hair. . . . He also sometimes used to punish his body with whips, the cords knotted" (quoted in Hexter, *More's "Utopia,"* p. 88).

APPENDIX

On Hexter's Account of More's Visit
to Antwerp in 1515

In a letter dated from London, 3 September 1516, More tells that he sent a completed copy of the *Utopia* to Erasmus in Antwerp, "with a prefatory epistle to my friend Peter" (Erasmus, *Opus Epistolarum*, Vol. 2, p. 339). The prefatory epistle begins: "I am almost ashamed, my dear Peter Giles, to send you this little book about the state of Utopia after almost a year when I am sure you looked for it within a month and a half" (39/3-5). From a simple reading of the evidence of the *Utopia*, where More tells us that he made only one visit to Antwerp during the recess in the negotiations in the summer of 1515 (47/30-49/16), this would mean that he thought that Giles had every reason to expect that the *Utopia* would have been written within a month and a half of the end of the visit when they first met each other and had, in their conversations, developed not only the broad outlines but also many of the details of Raphael's account which More had then offered or agreed to write down in book form.

Hexter has collected evidence (Yale ed., Appendix A, pp. 573-76) which points out that if, as More says, he had been away from his family for over four months at the time of his meeting with Giles (49/15-16)—which would put the date around 12 September 1515, since we know that he left England about 12 May (p. 573)—then, because he wrote the work "at leisure" (Erasmus, *Epistles*, Vol. 3, p. 389), of which he had none after returning to England soon after 21 October (p. 574), we are forced to ask whether he was ever at leisure in the Netherlands between 12 September and 21 October. Hexter goes on to suggest that More's known activities after mid-September were so full that "At this point the question of whether in these conditions More could be said to have written the Discourse at leisure seems to be superseded by the question of whether under such circumstances and limitations he could have written it at all'' (p. 574).

Hexter thinks not, and supposes instead that More in fact made *two* visits to Giles in Antwerp: the first, following the recess in the negotiations (after 21 July), when he and Giles had the conversations which led to writing the Discourse (p. xxxi), and a second time, around 12 September (which explains More's statement that he was at Giles' when he was four months away from home). At this second visit, Hexter surmises, More took Giles "the nearly complete rough draft of what became the Introduction and Discourse on Utopia" (p. xxxiii), and it was this, polished and completed, which he had every reason to expect "within a month and a half." Hexter's supposition (and he does not present it as anything more, see p. 576, last sentence) depends on judgements about (i) what Erasmus meant by More's "leisure," and (ii) what More could be thought to have done "at leisure" between 12 September and 21 October in 1515. There are several points which make me reject Hexter's suppositions for the simpler one-visit reading which accords with the evidence we have from More.

First, Hexter himself allows that the first "nearly complete rough draft" which More took to Giles in September (and which needed only six weeks to be polished and copied, p. xxii) would in any case have been written in six weeks. If we follow Hexter's proposal, More went first from Bruges to Antwerp soon after 21 July, stayed there on business, met and talked with Giles for, say (?), one week before returning to Bruges by, say (?), 1 August, where, on Hexter's supposition, he must have written the Introduction and Discourse in the *remaining six weeks* before returning with it, to Giles, in Antwerp by 12 September. In either view then, the work was substantially *written in six weeks*. The whole question is whether it could have been written "at leisure" in the six weeks after More's visit to Giles in mid-September or, as Hexter would have it, in the six weeks from 1 August to mid-September.

Hexter lists three things More is thought to have done after 12 September which make him doubt that he "could have written it at all"—much less "at leisure"—after this date. They are (i) doing a "considerable part of the writing on the long letter to Dorp," (ii) "taking care of whatever business (*res*, 46/29) had taken him to Antwerp," and (iii) "winding up any business that his duties as emissary entailed" (p. 574).

There is no reason to suppose that the second amounted to anything very time-consuming (see Surtz's suggestions in the Yale ed., p. 300, 48/13). In any event, according to Hexter's own argument, More could have looked after this business on his "first" visit and its mention in *Utopia* in connection with the visit in September could then be explained by Hexter's principle that More "telescoped the two visits" (p. 576).

The third point, that after 12 September More's time would have been consumed by winding up his official duties, is not very weighty. Surtz has shown that these amounted to nothing or very little. As he writes, "Existing letters from 1515 . . . show that More did not at all figure prominently in the negotiations. The active conduct of the affair was evidently in the hands of Tunstal, Sampson, Spinelly, and later Knight. It is necessary to conclude that More and Clifford were on the commission chiefly in an advisory capacity. Independently of the mention of his name in the commissions issued on May 7, 1515, and October 2, 1515, More's signature was affixed to only two surviving letters, those of July 9 and July 21, 1515" ("St. Thomas More and his Utopian Embassy of 1515," p. 295). There is no evidence that after 21 July More was at all busy with duties connected with the embassy.

As to the first point, More's composing of the letter to Dorp, Hexter himself supposes that he could very well have written part of it before he went to see Giles on 12 September—see p. 576 (Dorp's letter against Erasmus is dated 27 August 1515). If part was written *before* the September visit to Giles and part after, then the distinction between More's free time in the two six-week periods becomes less and less.

There is another point which could prove to be decisive. Hexter's whole chronology depends on the assumption that the date More is known to have left England, "about May 12, 1515" (p. 573), is identical to the start of the time More refers to when he says that, while with Giles in Antwerp, he had been more than four months separated "from my home, my wife, and children" (49/14—the words used for "home," *ac laris domestici*, indicate his actual house, not England). It is possible that the preparation for the embassy kept More, though still in London, substantially away from his family for a couple of weeks prior to his departure in which case he could have been with Giles as early as the beginning of September and still be correct when he says that he had been away *from his family* for more than four months—which is what he actually says and not, as Hexter reads it, *away from England*. If this could be shown then we would also save the accuracy of this statement to Erasmus (Erasmus, *Epistles*, 2, 195-96), that the Netherlands mission occupied him for "more than six months"—i.e., from about 28 April to the end of October. Hexter dismisses this statement as a sloppy remark of one "not in any case beset by any consuming passion for chronological accuracy" (p. 576, n. 1), thinking only of the journey itself which lasted from mid-May until the end of October.

Finally, Hexter begins his argument by ruling out any suggestion that More could have stayed in Antwerp from soon after the recess in the negotiations on 21 July until 12 September. More's words in *Utopia* are "Meanwhile, as my business led me, I made my way to Antwerp. While I stayed there, among my other visitors . . . was Peter Giles" (47/30-49/2). Hexter says, "To stretch that 'meanwhile' up to a point at least fifty-four days later in order to fit it to More's other statement [four months from his family] is to put more than a considerable strain on it" (p. 573). I do not see why this is so. There is no evidence to suggest that More was anywhere other than at Antwerp in the period between the end of July and 12 September—with the exception of a brief visit to Tournai on Erasmus' account (p. 575). I suggest that we should therefore leave him in Antwerp for the whole period and perhaps beyond. In this case he would have had ample time and leisure to become friends with Giles, have had the conversations which worked out the Utopian institutions, and have done however much of the writing as was consistent with Giles getting a finished copy within six weeks of the time the two friends parted—which, for all we know, could have been as late as mid-October.

BIBLIOGRAPHY

The following is a list of the works cited and the editions consulted. For ancient and patristic sources I have not referred to the critical editions but only to commonly accessible texts.

Adams, R. P. *The Better Part of Valor: More, Erasmus, Colet, and Vives on Humanism, War, and Peace, 1496-1535*. Seattle, University of Washington Press, 1962.

Allen, J. W. *A History of Political Thought in the Sixteenth Century*. 1928. London, Methuen, 1957.

Allen, P. R. "*Utopia* and European Humanism: The Function of the Prefatory Letters and Verses." *Studies in the Renaissance*, 10 (1963).

Ambrose. *Letters*. Trans. H. de Romestin et al. In *Nicene and Post-Nicene Fathers*. 2nd series. Vol. 10. Grand Rapids, Mich., Wm. B. Eerdmans, 1955.

Ames, Russell. *Citizen Thomas More and His Utopia*. Princeton, Princeton University Press, 1949.

Aristotle. *Metaphysica*. Trans. W. D. Ross. 2nd ed. Oxford, Clarendon Press, 1928.

_____ . *Politics*. Trans. Ernest Barker. Oxford, Oxford University Press Paperback, 1958.

Augustine. *City of God*. Trans. H. Bettenson. Harmondsworth, Penguin Books, 1972.

_____ . *Confessions*. Trans. R. S. Pine-Coffin. Harmondsworth, Penguin Books, 1972.

Baker-Smith, D. *Thomas More and Plato's Voyage*. An Inaugural Lecture given on 1 June 1978 at University College, Cardiff. Cardiff, University College Cardiff Press, 1978.

Beger, Lina. "Thomas Morus und Platon: Ein Betrag zur Geschichte des Humanismus." *Zeitschrift für die gesammte Staatswessenschaft* (Tübingen), 35 (1897).

Booth, W. C. *The Rhetoric of Fiction*. Chicago, University of Chicago Press, 1961.

Bradshaw, Brendan. "More on Utopia." *The Historical Journal*, 24 (1981).

Brewer, J. S. et al., eds. *Letters and Papers, Foreign and Domestic, of the Reign of Henry VIII*. 21 vols. Records Office, London, 1862-1932.

Bridgett, T. E. *The Life and Writings of Blessed Thomas More*. London, Burns, Oates & Washbourne, 1924.

Carlyle, R. W., and A. J. Carlyle. *A History of Medieval Political Thought in the West*. Vols. 4 and 5. Edinburgh and London, William Blackwood & Sons, 1930.

Cassirer, Ernst. *The Platonic Renaissance in England*. Trans. J. P. Pettegrove. 1932. New York, Thomas Nelson & Sons, 1953.

Chambers, R. W. *Thomas More*. The Bedford Historical Series. London, Jonathan Cape, 1935.

Cicero. *De Officiis*. Trans. Walter Miller. Loeb Classical Library. Cambridge, Mass., Harvard University Press, 1913.

Cross, R. C., and A. D. Woozley. *Plato's Republic, A Philosophical Commentary*. London, Macmillan, 1964.

Dante. *The Divine Comedy*. Text with translation and commentary by Charles S. Singleton. Bollingen Series LXXX. Princeton, Princeton University Press, 1970-75.

Descartes, René. *Philosophical Works*. Trans. E. S. Haldane and G. R. T. Ross. 2 vols. Cambridge, Cambridge University Press, 1973.

Diogenes Laertius. *Lives of Eminent Philosophers*. Trans. R. D. Hicks. 2 vols. Rev. ed. Loeb Classical Library. Cambridge, Mass., Harvard University Press, 1972.

Duhamel, P. Albert. "Medievalism in More's *Utopia*." *Studies in Philology*, 52 (1955).

Epstein, P. "Law and Subjective Freedom in *The Merchant of Venice*." *Dionysius*, 7 (1983).

Erasmus. *The Complaint of Peace*. Trans. T. Paynell [?]. Chicago: Open Court Publishing, 1917.

———. *The Correspondence of Erasmus*. Trans. R. A. B. Mynors and D. F. S. Thomson. In *The Collected Works of Erasmus*. Toronto, University of Toronto Press, 1987- . Cited as *Correspondence*.

———. *The Education of a Christian Prince*. Trans. L. K. Born. Records of Civilization, Sources and Studies. 1936. New York, W. W. Norton, 1968.

———. *The Epistles of Erasmus, from His Earliest Letters to His Fifty-first Year*. Trans. F. M. Nichols. 3 vols. New York, Russell & Russell, 1962. The title page of Vol. 3 extends the scope to his fifty-third year. Cited as *Epistles*.

———. *Opus Epistolarum Des. Erasmi Roterodami*. Ed. P. S. Allen. 12 vols. Oxford, Clarendon Press, 1906-58. Cited as *Opus Epistolarum*.

———. *In Praise of Folly*. Trans. J. Wilson. 1668. Ann Arbor, University of Michigan Press, Ann Arbor Paperbacks, 1958.

Gadamer, H.-G. *Dialogue and Dialectic: Eight Hermeneutical Studies on Plato*. Trans. P. C. Smith. New Haven, Yale University Press, 1980.

Goldschmidt, V. *Platonisme et pensée contemporaine*. Paris, Aubier, éditions Montaigne, 1970.

Gordon, W. M. "The Monastic Achievement and More's Utopian Dream." *Medievalia et Humanistica*, New Series, 9 (1979).

Graesse, J. G. T. *Trésor des livres rares et précieux*. Milan, Ricordari, 1950.

Grant, George. *Technology and Empire*. Toronto, House of Anansi, 1969.

Hegel, G. W. F. *The Philosophy of History*. Trans. J. Sibree. 1899. New York, Dover Publications, 1956.

Heiserman, A. R. "Satire in the *Utopia*." *PMLA*, 78 (1963).

Heresbach, Conrad. *De educandis atque erudiendis principium liberis....* Torgau, 1598.

Hesiod. *Works and Days*. In *The Homeric Hymns and Homerica* Trans. Hugh G. Evelyn-White. Loeb Classical Library. Cambridge, Mass., Harvard University Press, 1914.

Hexter, J. H. *More's "Utopia": The Biography of an Idea*. 1952. Repr. with an epilogue, New York, Harper Torchbooks, 1965.

Hobbes, Thomas. *Leviathan*. Ed. M. Oakeshott. Blackwell's Political Texts. Oxford, Basil Blackwell, n.d.

––––––––. *Elements of Law*. Ed. Ferdinand Tönnies. Cambridge, 1928.

Horace. *Carmina*. In *Odes and Epodes*. Trans. C. E. Bennett. Loeb Classical Library. Cambridge, Mass., Harvard University Press, 1914.

Huizinga, J. *Erasmus and the Age of Reformation*. Trans. F. Hopman. 1924. New York: Harper & Row, 1957.

––––––––. *The Waning of the Middle Ages*. Trans. F. Hopman. 1924. Garden City, N.Y., Doubleday Anchor Books, 1954.

Isocrates. *To Nicocles*. In *Isocrates*. Vol. 1. Trans. G. Norlin. Loeb Classical Library. Cambridge, Mass., Harvard University Press, 1928.

Justinian. *Pandects* or *Digest* (in the *Corpus Juris Civilis*). Ed. T. Mommsen. Trans. C. H. Munro. 2 vols. Berlin, 1870. Cambridge, 1904-1909.

Kautsky, Karl. *Thomas More and His Utopia*. 1st German ed., 1888. Trans. H. J. Stenning. 1927. Repr. with a foreword by Russell Ames. New York, Russell & Russell, 1959.

Kempis, Thomas à. *The Imitation of Christ*. Trans. Richard Whitford. Ed. Harold C. Gardiner. 1530. Garden City, N.Y., Image Books, 1955.

Kristeller, Paul Oskar. *The Philosophy of Marsilio Ficino*. Trans. V. Conant. New York: Columbia University Press, 1943.

––––––––. *Renaissance Thought: The Classic, Scholastic and Humanist Strains*. New York: Harper Torchbooks, 1962.

Kurth, Willi. *The Complete Woodcuts of Albrecht Dürer*. New York: Dover Publications, 1963.

Lewis, C. S. *English Literature in the Sixteenth Century, Excluding Drama*. The Oxford History of English Literature, 3. Oxford, Clarendon Press, 1954.

Lewis, C. T., and C. Short. *A Latin Dictionary*. Oxford, Clarendon Press, 1969.

Liddell, H. G., and R. Scott. *Abridged Greek-English Lexicon*. Oxford: Clarendon Press, 1871.

––––––––. *A Greek-English Lexicon*. With a Supplement. Oxford, Clarendon Press, 1968.

Livy. *Ab Urbe Condita*. In *Livy*. Trans. B. O. Foster et al. 13 vols. plus Index vol. Loeb Classical Library. Cambridge, Mass., Harvard University Press, 1919- .

Locke, John. *Essay Concerning Human Understanding*. Ed. A. C. Fraser. 1894. 2 vols. New York: Dover Publications, 1959.

Logan, G. M. *The Meaning of More's "Utopia."* Princeton, Princeton University Press, 1983.

Lot, Ferdinand. *The End of the Ancient World and the Beginnings of the Middle Ages*. Trans. P. and M. Leon. 1931. New York: Harper Torchbooks, 1961.

Lucian. *Lucian*. Trans. A. M. Harmon et al. 8 vols. Loeb Classical Library. Cambridge, Mass., Harvard University Press, 1913- .

Lupton, J. H. *A Life of John Colet . . . with an Appendix of Some of His English Writings*. London, 1887. 2nd ed. Hamden, Conn., Shoe String Press, 1961.

Luther, Martin. *The Babylonian Captivity of the Church*. In *Three Treatises, Martin Luther*. From the American edition of *Luther's Works*, Vol. 36, trans. A. T. W. Steinhäuser, rev. Frederick C. Ahrens and Abdel Ross Wentz. Philadelphia, Fortress Press, 1960.

————. *Secular Authority: To What Extent It Should Be Obeyed*. Trans. J. J. Schindel. In *Works of Martin Luther*. Vol. 3. Philadelphia, A. J. Holman Co. and Castle Press, 1930.

Machiavelli, Niccolò. *The Discourses of Niccolò Machiavelli*. Trans. Leslie J. Walker. London: Routledge & Kegan Paul, 1953.

————. *The Prince, A Bilingual Edition*. Trans. and ed. Mark Musa. New York, St. Martin's Press, 1964.

Manuel, F. E., and F. P. Manuel. *Utopian Thought in the Western World*. Cambridge, Mass., Harvard University Press, 1979.

McCutcheon, Elizabeth. "Thomas More, Raphael Hythlodaeus, and the Angel Raphael." *Studies in English Literature*, 9 (1969).

More, Thomas. *Here is conteyned the lyfe of Johan Picus Erle of Myrandula . . . .* London, *c.* 1510. In *The workes of Sir Thomas More . . . wrytten by him in the Englysh tonge*. London, 1557. In *The English Works of Sir Thomas More, Reproduced in Facsimile from William Rastell's Edition of 1515 and Edited with a Modern Version of the Same by W. E. Campbell*. 2 vols. London, 1931.

————. *Latin Poems*. Ed. C. H. Miller, L. Bradner, C. A. Lynch and R. P. Oliver. In *The Complete Works of St. Thomas More*. Vol. 3, Part II. New Haven, Yale University Press, 1984.

————. *Opera*. Ed. G. J. Vossius. Amsterdam, 1695-1701.

————. *Translations of Lucian*. Ed. C. R. Thompson. In *The Complete Works of St. Thomas More*. Vol. 3, Part I. New Haven, Yale University Press, 1974.

————. *Utopia, The "Utopia" of Sir Thomas More*. Ed. J. H. Lupton. Oxford, Clarendon Press, 1895.

————. *Utopia*. Ed. A. G. M. De Querlon. London and Paris, 1777.

————. *Utopia*. Ed. Edward Surtz, S.J. and J. H. Hexter. In *The Complete Works of St. Thomas More*. Vol. 4. New Haven, Yale University Press, 1965.

————. *Utopia*. Trans. with an Introduction by Paul Turner. Harmondsworth, Penguin Books, 1965.

Morrison, Samuel Eliot. *The European Discovery of America: The Southern Voyages A.D. 1942-1616*. New York, Oxford University Press, 1974.

Oncken, Hermann. "Introduction" to *Utopia*. Ed. with German trans. by Gerhard Ritter. Berlin, R. Hobbing, 1922.

Parks, G. B. "More's Utopia and Geography." *Journal of English and Germanic Philology*, 37 (1938).

Petrarch. *Africa*. Ed. L. Pingaud. Paris, 1872.

Plato. *Apology. Cratylus. Laws. Sophist. Statesman. Republic*. In *The Collected Dialogues of Plato*. Ed. Edith Hamilton and Huntington Cairns. Bollingen Series LXXI. Princeton, Princeton University Press, 1961.

Popper, Karl R. *The Open Society and Its Enemies*. 2 vols. 5th ed. rev. Princeton, Princeton University Press, 1966.

Quarta, Cosimo. *L'Utopia platonica, il projetto politico di un grande filosofo*. Milano, Italia, F. Angeli, 1985.

Roper, William. *The Lyfe of Sir Thomas More*. Ed. E. V. Hitchcock. Oxford, Early English Text Society, 1935.

Ross, W. D. *Plato's Theory of Ideas*. Oxford, Clarendon Press, 1951.

Sabine, G. H. *A History of Political Theory*. New York, Holt, Rinehart & Winston, 1937.

Sallust. *Bellum Catilinae*. In *Sallust*. Trans. J. C. Rolfe. Loeb Classical Library. Rev. ed. Cambridge, Mass., Harvard University Press, 1931.

Schaeffer, J. D. "Socratic Method in More's *Utopia*." *Moreana*, 69 (1981).

Scullard, H. H. *A History of the Roman World 753-146 B.C.* 4th ed. London and New York, Methuen, 1980.

Seyssel, Claude de. *La Monarchie de France*. Ed. Jacques Poujol. Paris, 1961.

Shakespeare, W. *The Tempest*. In *The Works of William Shakespeare Gathered into One Volume*. The Shakespeare Head Press Edition. New York, Oxford University Press, n.d.

Skinner, Quentin. *The Foundations of Modern Political Thought*. Vol. 1. Cambridge, Cambridge University Press, 1978.

Stapleton, Thomas. *The Life and Illustrious Martyrdom of Sir Thomas More*. Trans. Philip E. Hallett. 1928. Stapleton-Hallett, ed. E. E. Reynolds. London, Burns & Oates, 1966.

Starnes, C. J. *Augustine's Conversion: A Commentary on the Argument of Books I-IX of the* Confessions. Waterloo, Ontario, Wilfrid Laurier University Press, forthcoming, 1990.

_____ . "Augustinian Biblical Exegesis and the Origins of Modern Science." Forthcoming in *Collectanea Augustiniana*.

Strauss, Leo. *Studies in Platonic Political Philosophy*. Chicago, University of Chicago Press, 1983.

_____ . *Natural Right and History*. Chicago, University of Chicago Press, 1953.

Surtz, E. "St. Thomas More and his Utopian Embassy of 1515." *Catholic Historical Review*, 39 (1953).

Taylor, A. E. *Plato, the Man and His Work*. 7th ed. London, Methuen, University Paperbacks, 1966.

Tierney, Brian. *The Crisis of Church and State: 1050-1300*. Englewood Cliffs, N.J., Prentice-Hall, 1964.

Vergil. *Aeneid*. Ed. R. A. B. Mynors. Oxford Classical Texts, reprinted with corrections. Oxford, Clarendon Press, 1972.

_____ . *Aeneid*. Trans. Robert Fitzgerald. New York, Random House, 1983.

Vespucci, Amerigo. *Mundus Novus*. Basle, 1505. Repr., *Mundus Novus: Letter to Lorenzo Pietro di Medici*. Trans. G. T. Northup. Princeton, 1916.

_____ . *Quatuor Americi Vespucij navigationes*. St. Die, 1507. Repr. in *The Cosmographiae Introductio of Martin Waldseemüller in Facsimile, Followed by the Four Voyages of Amerigo Vespucci, with their Translation into English*. Ed. C. G. Herbermann. Trans. Mario E. Cosenza. Monograph 4. New York, U.S. Catholic Historical Society, 1907.

Vincent of Lerins. *Commonitorium*. Ed. R. S. Moxon. Cambridge Patristic Texts, 1915. Trans. A. C. Heurtley. In *Nicene and Post Nicene Fathers*. 2nd series. Vol. 11. Grand Rapids, Mich., Wm. B. Eerdmans, 1955.

Volgin, V. "Sir Thomas More." *News, A Review of World Events*, 39 (15 February 1953). Reprinted in L. Gallagher, *More's Utopia and its Critics*. Chicago, Scott, Foresman, 1964.

Wells, H. G. "Introduction to *Utopia*. Limited Editions Club. New York, Heritage Press, 1935.

White, N. P. *A Companion to Plato's* Republic. Indianapolis, Hackett, 1979.

White, Thomas I. "Pride and the Public Good: Thomas More's Use of Plato in *Utopia*." *Journal of the History of Philosophy*, 20, 4 (October 1982).

Williams, George Hunston. *Wilderness and Paradise in Christian Thought*. New York, Harper, 1962.

Xenophon. *Cyropaedia*. Trans. W. Miller. 2 vols. Loeb Classical Library. Cambridge, Mass., Harvard University Press, 1914.

INDEX